DATE DUE			

363.73   Tesar, Jenny E.   5320
TES
         Global warming.

MESA VERDE MIDDLE SCHOOL
POWAY UNIFIED SCHOOL DISTRICT

350148 02047   03328A   04

OUR FRAGILE PLANET

GLOBAL WARMING

Jenny Tesar

Series Editor:
Bernard S. Cayne

A Blackbirch Graphics Book

Facts On File
New York

MESA VERDE MIDDLE SCHOOL
8375 ENTREKEN WAY
SAN DIEGO, CA 92129

Copyright © 1991 by Blackbirch Graphics, Inc.
Text copyright © 1991 by Jenny Tesar
All rights reserved. No part of this book may be reproduced or utilized in any form or by any means, electronic or mechanical, including photocopying, recording, or by any information storage or retrieval systems, without permission in writing from the publisher. For information contact:
Facts On File, Inc.
460 Park Avenue South
New York, NY 10016
USA

Library of Congress Cataloging-in-Publication Data
Tesar, Jenny E.
  Global warming.
  (Our fragile planet/by Jenny Elizabeth Tesar; series editor, Bernard S. Cayne.)
  Includes bibliographical references and index.
  Summary: Discusses the gradual warming of our planet, its possible causes and effects, and some solutions.
  ISBN 0-8160-2490-1
  1. Global warming—Juvenile literature. 2. Environmental protection—United States—Juvenile literature. [1. Global warming.] I.Title. II. Series: Tesar, Jenny E. Our fragile planet.
QC981.8.G56T47 1991
363.73'87—dc20
                                                                90-47544

A British CIP catalogue record for this book is available from the British Library.

Facts On File books are available at special discounts when purchased in bulk quantities for businesses, associations, institutions or sales promotions. Please call our Special Sales Department in New York at 212/683-2244 (dial 800/322-8755 except in NY, AK, or HI) or in Oxford at 865/728399.

Design: Blackbirch Graphics, Inc.

Printed and Manufactured in the United States of America.

10 9 8 7 6 5 4 3 2

This book is printed on acid-free paper.

Contents

Chapter 1	The Greenhouse Effect	5
Chapter 2	An Ocean of Air	11
Chapter 3	Carbon Dioxide in the Atmosphere	21
Chapter 4	Human Activity and Carbon Dioxide Levels	27
Chapter 5	Heat Traps	35
Chapter 6	A Hole in the Sky	41
Chapter 7	Predicting the Future	49
Chapter 8	Effects of Rising Temperatures	57
Chapter 9	Adapting to Changes	73
Chapter 10	The Need to Conserve Energy	81
Chapter 11	Slowing the Warming Trend	97
	Glossary	106
	Further Reading	108
	Index	110

1
THE GREENHOUSE EFFECT

Monday was the hottest day on record. People stayed in, turned up the air conditioners, and ate salads instead of hot-cooked meals. Sidewalks and gardens were deserted. Shopping malls and movie houses enjoyed increased business—so did ice-cream vendors.

Tuesday was worse. The temperature rose to a new high. Several people died because of the heat. Other heat victims filled hospital emergency rooms. Cars stopped running as their radiators overheated. The glue on golf clubs melted, causing the heads to fall off. Video tapes warped. Concrete buckled. For 90 minutes, airplane flights were cancelled because temperatures passed the maximum levels foreseen in operation manuals, causing pilots to fear that there wouldn't be enough lift for takeoff.

Is this a scene from a science fiction tale set in an imagined future? No. It was a scene in Phoenix, Arizona, in June 1990. During an unprecedented heat wave, temperatures hit 122°F (50°C). Other communities in the American Southwest also experienced record-breaking temperatures. In Texas, road pavers labored in "pretty rough working conditions" as the asphalt they were using reached 380°F (193°C). In Los Angeles, increased use of air conditioners pushed electricity use to an all-time high of more than 5,000 megawatts.

Is this a forecast of things to come? Many scientists believe so. They predict that within the next few decades, the Earth's

Opposite page: Carbon dioxide traps heat in the Earth's atmosphere and raises global temperatures, just as temperatures rise when heat is trapped inside a greenhouse.

climate will be warmer than at any time in the past 1,000 years. By the middle of the next century, it may be warmer than at any time in the past 125,000 years.

These predictions are based on changes in the atmosphere—changes that are occurring because of human activities: driving cars, running air conditioners, raising cattle, cutting down forests, turning on lights, making computers, operating steel mills, growing rice, baking pies, flying airplanes, burning wood, manufacturing soda cans, ironing clothes, making ice cubes—the list goes on and on. Every aspect of human society is involved: homes, schools, offices, hospitals, stores, restaurants, factories and farms.

The problem is that we are pouring huge amounts of carbon dioxide and other heat-trapping gases into the atmosphere. These gases are acting much like the glass in a greenhouse. Glass allows solar energy to enter the greenhouse but prevents heat energy from escaping. Similarly, heat-trapping gases in the atmosphere allow most of the sun's energy to reach the Earth's surface but prevent heat given off by the Earth from escaping into space. As more and more heat is given off, the atmosphere becomes warmer and warmer. This phenomenon has been given a name: the greenhouse effect.

"The greenhouse effect is not a wild idea; it's pretty basic physics," says meteorologist Elmer Robinson, director of the Mauna Loa Observatory in Hawaii.

It's not a bad idea either, within limits. Without the heat-trapping ability of naturally occurring carbon dioxide, the Earth would be a very cold place. It would have an average surface temperature of only 0°F (−18°C). Instead, its average surface temperature is a balmy 59°F (15°C).

Our Global Laboratory

Scientists generally agree that increases in heat-trapping gases in the atmosphere will cause the average temperature of the Earth to rise by 3° to 8°F (1.7° to 4.4°C) within the next 60 years. In terms of the Earth's history, this would be a phenomenally rapid change.

It is not simply a matter of adding a few degrees to the average temperature of your community. A rise of this mag-

MARCH OF THE KUDZU

A huge green vine creeps over the land. It covers cars, trees, utility poles, houses and anything else in its path. People hack at it. They spray it with chemical weed killers. They try to dig up the enormous roots. They send in goats and cows to eat it. But they can't eradicate it. It keeps on spreading.

The vine is the kudzu. A native of Japan, it was introduced in the United States at the 1876 Centennial Exposition in Philadelphia. The Japanese used one of the plants to decorate their exhibit at the exposition. Americans admired the vine, which has large, grassy green leaves and clusters of beautiful purple flowers. They asked the Japanese for seeds to plant in their gardens.

In Japan, the kudzu has natural enemies that limit its growth. Cold winters kill the vines, even though the roots remain alive. But in the American South, there are no natural enemies, no killing frosts. The kudzu grows and grows and grows. Its roots can weigh as much as 400 pounds (180 kilograms). As many as 50 vines may grow from a single root—and each vine may be 100 feet (30 meters) long.

Today, the kudzu is a common weed from Florida to Texas. It is found as far north as southern Pennsylvania. But in the coming years people even further north may be joining the battle against the kudzu. If the greenhouse effect causes temperatures to rise, the kudzu may spread into New England, Indiana, Illinois and Michigan. This is but one small example of the changes that may occur as the Earth warms.

---

nitude will affect every aspect of our environment, including weather patterns, polar ice caps, ocean levels and the habitats of plants and animals.

Changing weather patterns, for example, will mean that some places will receive more rain than they do today, while other places will become much drier. Warming seas will expand and polar ice caps will melt. This means that coastal areas will be flooded, perhaps permanently. In turn, such changes will affect farms, beaches, wetlands, forests, cities—every type of habitat, every type of community. "There will be no winners in this game of ecological chairs, for it will be fundamentally disruptive and destabilizing," said biologist Thomas Lovejoy of the Smithsonian Institution.

Scientists base their predictions on a broad range of evidence. Arctic ice samples show changes in carbon dioxide levels that have occurred over the past 10,000 years. Monitoring stations around the world gather data on current levels of greenhouse gases. Highly complex computer programs simulate the effects on atmospheric temperatures as more and more of these gases are pumped into the air.

But it is impossible to set up a laboratory or design a computer program that reproduces all of the forces that govern our planet. Scientists still do not understand all the interrelationships among different parts of the atmosphere. Nor do they understand all the interrelationships between the atmosphere and the oceans, forests, ice caps and other parts of the Earth's surface.

So the Earth becomes our laboratory—which means that we will not know the specific results of dumping huge amounts of pollutants into the sky until they actually happen. We won't know exactly what amount of temperature change will occur, when it will occur, how it will affect climate and oceans and land until these things actually happen.

Will it be possible for humans to prevent some or all of the global warming from taking place? Perhaps. Will humans and other organisms be able to adjust to any changes that do occur? Perhaps. Much depends on what actions we take, now

TIMELINE

1800 American-British scientist Benjamin Thompson (Count) Rumford explained the basic physics of ocean circulation.
German-British astronomer Sir Frederick Herschel discovered infrared radiation.

1801 German physicist Johann W. Ritter discovered ultraviolet radiation.

1861 British physicist John Tyndall theorized that gases in the atmosphere were keeping the Earth warm.

1896 Swedish scientist Svante Arrhenius discovered that carbon dioxide traps enough reflected heat to warm the Earth's surface. He estimated that a doubling of carbon dioxide levels could warm the planet more than 10° F (5.5° C).

1899 American geologist Thomas C. Chamberlin also observed that carbon dioxide contributes to maintaining heat balance and that changes in the amount of carbon dioxide could affect the Earth's temperature.
French meteorologist Leon Philippe Teisserenc de Bort discovered the stratosphere.

1928 The radiosonde, an instrument package with a radio transmitter, was introduced.
American chemist Thomas Widgley Jr. invented Freon, the first chlorofluorocarbon (CFC).

1930 Meteorologist W. G. Kendrew likened the atmosphere "to the glass roof and sides of a hothouse [an early term for a greenhouse]."

1938 Nitrous oxide was discovered in the atmosphere.

1950s Scientists began to notice an increase in the acidity of lakes.

1957 American scientists Roger Revelle and Hans Suess warned that by adding carbon dioxide to the atmosphere, humans were conducting a "large-scale geophysical experiment."

1958 American atmospheric chemist Charles D. Keeling began the first modern carbon dioxide monitoring program atop Mauna Loa in Hawaii.

1959 Norwegian Fisheries Inspector A. Dannevig connected the decline in fish populations of Norwe-

and in the coming years. You, I, our neighbors, people all over the world—we're all in this together. We are all part of the problem. And part of the solution. One person's pollution and wastefulness may cause problems for other people. One community's lack of planning may affect other communities. One nation's continuing "business as usual" may create hardships for other nations.

Scientists stress that we face crucial, often extremely difficult decisions. The longer we wait, they say, the more difficult these decisions are likely to be—and the more likely that any actions we take will be too late.

"Worldwide action against the climatic threat is urgently required, even if the complicated scientific interrelationships of climatic change have not all been fully understood," stresses Klaus Töpfer, West Germany's Minister for the Environment. "Gaps in knowledge must not be used as an excuse for worldwide inaction."

---

gian and Swedish lakes to the increased acidity of precipitation.

1960 TIROS I, the first weather satellite, was launched by the United States.

1972 American ecologist Gene E. Likens introduced the term *acid rain*.

1973 British chemist James Lovelock, the first scientist to investigate the distribution of CFCs around the world, indicated that CFCs could become a significant contributor to the greenhouse effect.

1975 Atmospheric chemists F. Sherwood Rowland and Mario Molina warned that the ozone layer was threatened by CFCs.

Climatologists Syukuro Manabe and Richard Wetherald created a three-dimensional climate model to study the greenhouse effect.

Scientists gathered at Ohio State University for the First International Symposium on Acid Precipitation and the Forest Ecosystem.

1978 The United States banned the manufacture of CFCs for aerosol propellants.

1979 The Convention on Long Range Transboundary Air Pollution was signed by 34 member countries of the U.N. Economic Commission for Europe. It was the first broad international agreement covering acid rain.

1985 The British Antarctic Survey announced the presence of a "hole" in the ozone layer over Antarctica.

1987 F. Sherwood Rowland estimated that a single atom of chlorine could destroy 100,000 molecules of ozone.

Twenty-four nations and the European Community signed the Montreal Protocol on Substances that Deplete the Ozone Layer, which mandated 50% reductions in CFC production by 1998.

1988 Scientists reported that atmospheric ozone levels had declined over most of the world.

Sweden became the first nation to enact legislation freezing carbon dioxide emissions.

1989 The Noordwijk Declaration of Climate Change called for a stabilization of carbon dioxide emissions as soon as possible.

1990 Ninety-three nations agreed to stop production of CFCs and other ozone-destroying chemicals by year 2000.

At the Second World Climate Conference, 135 nations agreed to limit greenhouse gas production.

2
An Ocean of Air

Most of the time we forget that we live at the bottom of a deep ocean—an ocean of air called the atmosphere. Yet this ocean is essential for life on Earth. Without it, there would be no humans, animals or plants on Earth. The atmosphere contains gases needed by organisms for breathing and other essential life processes.

The atmosphere is important in other ways as well. It acts as a shield, protecting living things on the Earth from dangerous high-energy particles from outer space called cosmic rays. The atmosphere also protects us from deadly solar radiation. It absorbs some of the sun's radiation. This keeps the Earth at endurable temperatures, protecting us from extremes of heat and cold and from dramatic temperature changes between day and night, summer and winter.

Every day, millions of stone and iron meteors bombard the atmosphere. Without the atmosphere, these particles would rain down on the Earth. Instead, friction with the air produces so much heat that most meteors burn up, producing streaks of light that are sometimes called shooting stars.

The atmosphere carries sound waves, making it possible for us to hear voices and music. It also permits light waves to spread into places that would otherwise be dark. If there were no atmosphere, the sky above us would appear inky black. Blue daytime skies, red sunsets, even rainbows would not exist if there were no atmosphere.

Opposite page:
A massive volcanic eruption—like that on Mount St. Helens in May of 1980—can temporarily change weather patterns by spewing large quantities of ash into the atmosphere and blocking sunlight.

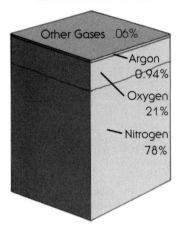

COMPOSITION OF AIR

Mixed Gases

Air is a mixture of different gases. These gases have weight, even though you cannot feel it. Hold out your hand palm up. If you are near sea level, you are holding about 250 pounds (113 kilograms) of the atmosphere in your palm! You do not feel the air pressing down on your hand because air pressure within your hand balances the external pressure.

The most abundant gas in the atmosphere is nitrogen. By volume, it comprises about 78% of the atmosphere. Oxygen is the second most abundant; it makes up 21% of the atmosphere. All the other gases combined make up less than 1%. They include argon (0.94%), carbon dioxide (0.03%), water vapor (0 to 4%) and trace gases. Trace gases are present in very tiny amounts. Helium, ozone, neon, methane, krypton, hydrogen and xenon are atmospheric trace gases.

Nitrogen

This element is a colorless, odorless gas that is needed by living things to form proteins. However, plants and animals cannot use the nitrogen in the atmosphere directly. First, the atmospheric nitrogen must be combined with other chemicals to form nitrates. This is done by nitrogen-fixing bacteria that live on the roots of certain legumes, such as alfalfa, beans, peas and clover. The nitrates they produce fertilize the soil. Plants absorb the nitrates and use them to make proteins. When animals eat the plants, the nitrogen passes into their bodies and is converted into animal proteins. When plants and animals decay, the nitrogen is returned to the atmosphere, thus completing the nitrogen cycle.

Oxygen

Each day, you breathe about 30 pounds (14 kilograms) of the atmosphere into and out of your lungs. Why? To obtain oxygen. This colorless, odorless gas is an element that almost all living things must have. You could live several weeks without food and several days without water, but several minutes without oxygen and you would be dead. All the cells of your body need oxygen to turn food into energy, in a process

THE TOOLS OF SCIENCE

People have been studying the atmosphere since ancient times. By the fifth century B.C., the Greeks were recording wind information and displaying this information for the benefit of sailors. About 300 B.C. the Greek naturalist Theophrastus wrote the *Book of Signs*, a collection of more than 200 natural signs that he thought were important indicators of weather. The book was used by weather forecasters for 2,000 years. In fact, some of Theophrastus's signs are still used today. The saying, "Red sky at morning, sailor take warning; red sky at night, sailor's delight" is derived from the *Book of Signs*.

Modern study of the atmosphere began in the 17th century, following the invention of two important instruments. Around the year 1610, Galileo Galilei, an Italian scientist, developed the first thermometer. And in 1643 Galileo's pupil Evangelista Torricelli invented the barometer, an instrument to determine atmospheric pressure. During the next two hundred years, other instruments were invented to measure wind speed and humidity, enabling people to observe all the basic ingredients of weather.

The development of large balloons during the 1800s gave scientists a tool to probe higher altitudes in the atmosphere. One result was the discovery of the stratosphere in 1899 by French meteorologist Teisserenc de Bort. In 1927, a balloon-borne instrument package and radio transmitter was developed. Called the radiosonde, it could radio back to Earth information on high-altitude air conditions. In the decades since then, increasingly sophisticated tools have been carried aloft by balloons, including telescopes, gas and isotope samplers and cosmic ray counters.

During World War II, bomber pilots added to our knowledge of the atmosphere with their discovery of jet streams—narrow bands of high-speed winds that circle the globe at an altitude of approximately 6 miles (10 kilometers).

Following the war, the United States used captured German V-2 rockets and, later, American-designed rockets to probe the atmosphere. An American Aerobee rocket was the first rocket to look down on a hurricane. Some rockets have been used to release chemicals into the upper atmosphere so that scientists could study the reactions of the gases there. And some have carried weather balloons as high as 200,000 feet (60,000 meters).

In 1960, the United States launched the first weather satellite, TIROS I (Television camera InfraRed Observational Satellite). The craft was equipped with a television camera that scanned the Earth and its atmosphere, sending back pictures of the cloud cover. For the first time, scientists were able to obtain a truly global view of the atmosphere.

Many satellites have since been launched to study atmospheric conditions. Cameras, radiation detectors and other instruments on the satellites detect, measure and radio back to Earth a broad range of data. Together with the development of high-speed computers, satellites and modern instrumentation have made it possible to construct mathematical models of atmospheric processes. This has greatly increased our understanding of what happens in the atmosphere and improved our ability to forecast the weather.

---

called respiration. In respiration, carbon dioxide is produced as a waste gas. It is breathed out, into the atmosphere.

Oxygen also makes fire possible. The combustion, or burning, of coal, oil, wood and other fuels takes place in the presence of oxygen. Combustion is much like the respiration that occurs in your body. Oxygen combines with the carbon in the fuel. Energy is released and carbon dioxide is produced as a waste product.

Carbon Dioxide

Carbon dioxide is another colorless, odorless gas in the atmosphere that is vital to life on Earth. It is needed by green plants to make food. In this process, oxygen is given off—oxygen that can be used by organisms for respiration.

Water Vapor

Unlike nitrogen and other components of the atmosphere, the amount of water in the atmosphere varies markedly from day to day and from place to place.

The amount of water in the air, expressed as a percentage of the maximum amount that the air could hold at a given temperature, is the relative humidity. For example, when the relative humidity is 70%, the air contains 70% of the moisture it is capable of holding at that temperature. When the relative humidity reaches 100%, water molecules condense on tiny particles in the atmosphere called cloud condensation nuclei. These include dust, sea salt, smoke and other particles.

The water in the atmosphere comes from the Earth's surface. It evaporates into the air from oceans, lakes, puddles, even your skin. Unlike other atmospheric components, water exists in the atmosphere not only as a gas but also in liquid and solid forms. Much is invisible water vapor. The rest condenses and freezes to form raindrops, snow and clouds. Whenever water changes from one form to another, heat is either given off or absorbed. During condensation and freezing, the water molecules give off heat, warming the surroundings. During evaporation and melting, water molecules absorb heat and cool the surroundings.

Most of the atmospheric water vapor is near the Earth's surface; the amount decreases rapidly with altitude.

A Warm Blanket

The sun is the source of virtually all the energy on our planet. Only a small portion reaches our atmosphere.

As solar radiation travels through the Earth's atmosphere, some of the radiation is reflected, or bounced off the air molecules back into space. Some is absorbed by the air molecules and changed to heat energy, thus warming the air. And some passes through the air to hit the surface of the Earth. On the average about 35% of the solar radiation is reflected back into space, about 18% is absorbed by the atmosphere and about 47% reaches the Earth's surface.

Radiation that reaches the Earth is absorbed by the ground and water. As a result, the Earth warms and some of the water evaporates. As the Earth's temperature rises, it radiates more and more heat upward into the atmosphere.

The heat energy radiated from the Earth is of longer wavelengths than the solar energy absorbed by the Earth. Energy of longer wavelengths does not pass easily back through the atmosphere. Much of it is absorbed by carbon dioxide, water and other molecules in the atmosphere. In turn, these molecules give off some of the heat that they have absorbed. Some is radiated upward and passes into outer space. But some is radiated downward and is absorbed by the Earth, adding to the heating of the surface.

In this manner, the atmosphere acts like an insulating blanket over the Earth. It prevents heat from being lost immediately to space. Rather, the heat energy is absorbed and then radiated back and forth between the atmosphere and the Earth a number of times before slowly filtering out into space. This keeps the Earth's surface warmer by about 60°F (33°C) than it would be if there were no atmosphere.

Dustlike Pollutants

The atmosphere contains countless tiny dust particles. These particles are so small and weigh so little that even slight air movements keep them aloft. You can see some of these particles when you look at a sunbeam. The sunbeam is actually the reflection of sunlight on the dust particles.

Dust can travel enormous distances. Most, however, is found in the air nearest the Earth's surface. In some places, particularly over large cities, there are so many particles that the air is dark. The particles screen out the sunlight, reflecting it back into space.

The most important function of dust particles is to serve as cloud condensation nuclei: centers around which water vapor can condense to form cloud particles. The result can often be seen over industrial cities where factories discharge large amounts of dust into the air. Moisture collects around the dust, forming a dense haze that hangs over the city.

Atmospheric dust comes from many different sources, both natural and human: erosion of rocks and soil, volcanic eruptions, forest fires, factory and ship smokestacks and so on.

Wind Action

As wind moves over the Earth's surface, it causes erosion. It rubs and polishes rocks, stones and other particles. The dust that is formed is fine enough to be carried aloft by the wind.

In deserts, where there are few or no plants, strong winds can lift huge quantities of dust into the air, forming a dense cloud called a dust storm. Dust storms can also occur where cultivation or overgrazing has stripped the ground of its protective plant cover. A dust storm that is 300 miles (483 kilometers) in diameter may carry enough dust to form a hill 100 feet (30 meters) high and 2 miles (3.2 kilometers) wide at the base!

As winds move over oceans and lakes, they lift up water droplets. Heavy droplets quickly fall back into the water. Smaller droplets remain aloft for a while and evaporate, leaving salt particles in the air.

Volcanoes

A volcanic eruption may inject immense quantities of dustlike particles called volcanic ash into the atmosphere. For example, when Mount St. Helens in Washington erupted on May 18, 1980, two columns of gas and steam loaded with ash shot more than 12 miles (19 kilometers) into the air.

Materials thrown into the lower atmosphere can have short-term effects on weather. Towns near Mount St. Helens experienced dramatically cooler days and warmer nights following the 1980 eruption. But temperatures returned to normal within a few days.

Particles ejected much higher into the atmosphere may take months or even years to spread out, or dissipate. In 1882, the violent eruption of Krakatoa on the island of Java sent enormous amounts of ash an estimated 30 miles (48 kilometers) into the air. British physicist Rollo Russell tracked the path of the ash cloud. He found that the cloud circled the Earth in two weeks—and then went around once again. Then the cloud spread out. Heavy particles gradually fell to earth. But tons of smaller particles remained in the atmosphere for many months, affecting weather around the world.

Other Sources
Every day, as much as 3,000 tons of dust fall into the Earth's atmosphere from outer space. As the particles drift slowly downward they are deposited on the Earth's surface. Many human activities emit particles into the air. Factories, refineries, incinerators, power plants, automobiles and airplanes—are just a few human sources of airborne particles. The atmosphere also contains many kinds of biological particles, including seeds, spores, pollen and tiny insects.

Layers of Air
The Earth's atmosphere is made up of four layers. Each layer is distinct. It differs from the others in temperature, density, composition and in the way it absorbs radiation from the sun. The altitude limits for each layer vary depending on geography and the season. All together, they envelop the Earth in a blanket some 300 miles (483 kilometers) thick.

Troposphere
The lowest layer—the one closest to the Earth—is called the troposphere. It is the home of all life. Even people who travel by air have never been beyond the troposphere, for the upper limit of this layer is about the limit to which commercial airplanes can fly.

Because of gravity, this is the densest layer of the atmosphere. About four-fifths of the atmosphere's mass is contained in the troposphere.

Air in the troposphere is heated primarily by the Earth's surface. Thus, the warmest air in the troposphere is that

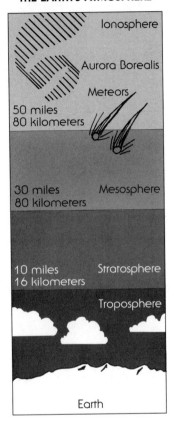

THE EARTH'S ATMOSPHERE

nearest the surface. When air molecules near the ground are heated, they rise. Cooler air sinks toward the ground and is heated. The amount of heat transferred from the surface to the air varies from place to place. As a result, winds form and the air is in constant motion. Hence the name *troposphere*, which comes from the Greek word *trope*, meaning the act of turning or changing. Almost all weather forms in this unstable layer: rainstorms, tornadoes, rainbows and so on. Most clouds are found in the troposphere.

If you have driven from a valley up to the top of a mountain, you probably noticed that the temperatures dropped as you went higher and higher. At ground level, the average temperature for the entire Earth is about 59° F (15° C). Of course, there are large departures from this average, depending on geographical location and season of the year. Everywhere, however, the average temperature decreases as the altitude increases. It falls about 3.5° F every 1,000 feet (6.4° C per kilometer). It continues falling to about 6.8 miles (11 kilometers), which is the upper boundary of the troposphere. Here, temperatures average about −70° F (−57° C).

The temperature then remains constant for several miles, in a region of transition called the tropopause.

Stratosphere

The layer of air above the tropopause is the stratosphere. It extends to a height of about 30 miles (48 kilometers). It is less dense than the underlying troposphere. Its composition is similar, however, except that there is much less water vapor and, therefore, fewer clouds.

Unlike the troposphere, temperatures increase with altitude in the stratosphere. This warming is caused by a layer of ozone. Ozone is a form of oxygen. The ozone absorbs most of the sun's ultraviolet radiation. This has two important effects. First, it warms the air in the stratosphere. Second, it prevents much of the ultraviolet radiation from reaching the Earth's surface. This is extremely important because ultraviolet radiation is harmful to living things, causing cancer and other health problems.

Temperatures rise in the stratosphere, reaching a high of about 29° F (−2° C). The point at which the temperature is highest marks the top of the stratosphere. Here again there is a transitional zone, called the stratopause, in which the temperature remains constant for several miles.

Mesosphere

Above the stratopause is the mesosphere. It lies between altitudes of approximately 30 and 53 miles (48 and 85 kilometers). The composition of the air is similar to that in the stratosphere. Some ozone is present. Water vapor is rare; if it is present it forms thin, feathery clouds of ice. The air is much thinner than in the stratosphere. The air molecules are so far apart that they cannot transmit sound; it is a silent world.

In the mesosphere, temperatures again decrease with height. At the highest altitude, temperatures may be below −103° F (−75° C). This is the lowest temperature in the atmosphere. This region of temperature minimum is called the mesopause.

Thermosphere

Above the mesopause is the thermosphere. Almost no water, carbon dioxide or ozone are found here. The air is very, very thin. Nonetheless, it is still dense enough to burn up meteors as they enter the atmosphere from outer space.

In the thermosphere, the temperature again increases with height. At the bottom of the layer, the temperature is below freezing. It rises to more than 2,000° F (1,100°C) at a height of 300 miles (483 kilometers). Because the air molecules are so far apart, they do not conduct, or pass on, this heat energy.

No sharp boundary marks the end of the thermosphere. The region immediately beyond the thermosphere is sometimes called the exosphere. Here, very thin air composed chiefly of hydrogen gradually merges with the gases of interplanetary space. The exposphere extends from about 300 miles (483 kilometers) to perhaps 2,000 miles (3,220 kilometers) above the Earth. This is the region in which communications and other useful satellites orbit our planet.

3
CARBON DIOXIDE IN THE ATMOSPHERE

Carbon dioxide comprises only a very small portion of the atmosphere—a little more than 0.03% by volume. This colorless, odorless gas is of vital importance to life on Earth. Indeed, without it, there probably would not be any plants or animals or human beings on our planet. But too much carbon dioxide could be as harmful as too little.

One important characteristic of carbon dioxide molecules is their ability to absorb heat energy. The greater the amount of carbon dioxide, the greater the amount of heat absorbed. The heat absorbed by the molecules remains in the atmosphere, rather than being radiated back into space. The result is higher temperatures on the Earth's surface and in the lower atmosphere.

There are many signs that the amount of carbon dioxide in the atmosphere is increasing. This threatens the balance between the amount of solar energy reaching Earth and the heat radiating outward from the Earth and its atmosphere.

Carbon Dioxide Captured by Plants

All living things need energy. The main source of energy is a simple sugar called glucose. When glucose is broken apart in the cells of an organism, energy is released. Where does the glucose come from? Directly or indirectly, all glucose comes from green plants.

Opposite page: Green plants differ from other living things in that they make their own food; through photosynthesis, they absorb light energy and produce glucose, a simple sugar.

IT'S ELEMENTARY

There are 92 natural chemical elements. Each kind of element has its own physical characteristics and its own chemical properties. Carbon (C), nitrogen (N), hydrogen (H), oxygen (O), iron (Fe) and helium (He) are examples of elements.

The basic building block of an element is the atom. One oxygen atom, for example, is represented by O. When atoms of an element are hooked together, a molecule is formed. For example, if two atoms of oxygen are connected, a molecule of oxygen gas (O_2) is produced. If three atoms of oxygen are connected, a molecule of ozone gas (O_3) is produced.

When two or more different kinds of elements combine chemically, compounds are formed. Water is a compound. It is composed of the elements hydrogen and oxygen. In each molecule of water there are two atoms of hydrogen and one atom of oxygen. This is written H_2O. A molecule of carbon dioxide contains one atom of carbon and two atoms of oxygen: CO_2. A molecule of carbonic acid contains two atoms of hydrogen, one atom of carbon and three atoms of oxygen. It is written H_2CO_3. If there are two molecules of carbonic acid, the formula is $2H_2CO_3$.

Green plants differ from other living things in one very important way: they can make their own food. The survival of other organisms depends on green plants. All animals feed either on plants or on animals that eat plants. The process by which green plants make food is called photosynthesis, a term derived from Greek words meaning "putting together with light." There are four basic requirements for photosynthesis: a source of energy, which usually is sunlight; water; carbon dioxide; and a green pigment called chlorophyll.

Foodmaking begins with the capture of light energy from the sun. The light energy is absorbed by the chlorophyll and used to break apart water molecules into hydrogen and oxygen. The oxygen is given off as waste. The hydrogen combines with carbon dioxide to form glucose. The process can be summarized by this equation:

$$\text{carbon dioxide} + \text{water} + \text{light energy}$$
$$(\text{in the presence of chlorophyll}) \rightarrow \text{glucose} + \text{oxygen}$$

$$6CO_2 + 6H_2O + \text{light} \rightarrow C_6H_{12}O_6 + 6O_2$$

The plants change some of the glucose into other carbohydrates. These include sugars other than glucose plus starches and celluloses. Some of the glucose is changed into more complex compounds such as proteins and fats. These are ultimately used by the plant for growth and energy.

Green plants convert huge amounts of carbon dioxide into food. It has been estimated that plants consume 500 billion tons of carbon dioxide every year, converting it and water into organic matter and oxygen.

Obviously, the larger the plant, the greater the amount of carbon stored in its tissues. A tree, which grows over many years, contains much, much more carbon than a soybean plant. A forest of trees stores millions of times more carbon than a field of soybeans. One of the biggest storehouses of carbon is in South America. The rain forest of the Amazon River basin covers 2.7 million square miles (7 million square kilometers) and stretches into nine countries. At least 75 billion tons of carbon are stored in the trees in this forest!

Eventually, most of the carbon is returned to the atmosphere or the oceans. The recycling of the carbon is extremely important. If this did not occur, soon there would be no carbon dioxide left for photosynthesis. Life would stop.

How is the carbon dioxide returned? The most important process is respiration. Some of the carbon compounds formed as a result of photosynthesis are broken down and burned in the plant cells for energy. This burning process is called respiration. In some ways, it is the reverse of photosynthesis:

$$\text{glucose} + \text{oxygen} \rightarrow \text{carbon dioxide} + \text{water} + \text{heat energy}$$

$$C_6H_{12}O_6 + 6O_2 \rightarrow 6CO_2 + 6H_2O + \text{heat}$$

Like the equation for photosynthesis, however, this is a very simple summary. Many complicated biochemical reactions occur during respiration.

Plants aren't the only organisms that respire. All organisms do. When green plants are eaten by animals, the carbon compounds in the plants are digested by the animals. Some of the digested foodstuffs are used to build and maintain body cells. Others are broken down into glucose and burned for energy, in the same respiration process found in plants.

When plant-eating animals are eaten by meat-eating animals, the same processes of digestion and respiration occur. In this way, carbon is transferred from one organism to another.

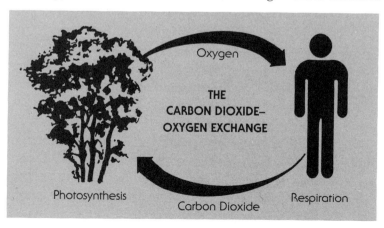

And much of it is exhaled back into the atmosphere as carbon dioxide, ready to be used by plants in photosynthesis.

When a plant or animal dies, bacteria and fungi feed on the remains. They digest the carbon compounds in the tissues of the dead organisms. This provides the energy they need to survive. And in the process, they too give off carbon dioxide.

The cycle is not in perfect balance. Not all plant and animal tissues are broken down. Some are trapped in the Earth and over long periods of time transformed into coal and other substances. Only when people burn these substances is the carbon released back into the atmosphere.

For instance, the coal we burn was formed from giant ferns and other plants that lived millions of years ago. When these plants died, their remains began to build up in swamps. More and more layers of decaying plants built up, one on top of the other. The great pressure of these layers changed the layers on the bottom into coal. In contrast, oil and gas deposits were formed from the remains of billions of tiny ocean organisms. As these organisms died, they dropped to the ocean bottom and were covered by mud. Many layers of mud accumulated in the course of time. Great pressure and heat gradually converted the mud into rock. And the plant and animal remains were transformed into petroleum and natural gas.

Carbon Dioxide Absorbed by Oceans

A photograph of the Earth taken from space provides dramatic evidence of just how much of our planet is water. About 70% of the Earth's surface is covered by oceans.

All the gases that make up the atmosphere are also dissolved in the oceans. The gases move back and forth between the atmosphere and the oceans. The proportions of these gases are not the same in the two places, however. Carbon dioxide, rather than nitrogen or oxygen, is the most abundant gas in ocean water.

Oceans absorb vast quantities of carbon dioxide from the atmosphere. It is not known exactly how much they absorb, nor how much they can absorb.

The atmosphere affects the temperature of the surface water. When the atmosphere is warm, the water is warmed

TOO COLD, TOO HOT

A look at Mars and Venus supports the general concept of the greenhouse theory. These planets are the Earth's closest planetary neighbors in the solar system. But their atmospheres are very different from our atmosphere. One is freezing cold, the other is boiling hot.

Mars has a thin atmosphere that is 95% carbon dioxide. But because there is so little air, the total amount of carbon dioxide is insufficient to trap much heat. Partly as a result of this, the planet has an average temperature of −76° F (−60° C). Scientists believe that if Mars had an atmosphere similar to that of the Earth, its average temperature would increase some 72° F (40° C).

The atmosphere surrounding Venus also consists almost entirely of carbon dioxide. It is a very dense atmosphere, however, able to trap enormous amounts of heat. As a result, Venus is excruciatingly hot, with an average surface temperature of 900° F (482° C). Part of this heat is due to the fact that Venus is closer to the sun and receives more solar energy. But if the Venusian atmosphere had the same carbon dioxide levels as Earth's atmosphere, the surface temperature would be around 356° F (180° C).

---

and its temperature rises. When the atmosphere is cold, the water cools. Warm water cannot hold as much dissolved gas as cold water. Thus, more carbon dioxide dissolves in cold ocean waters near the North and South poles.

The amount of carbon dioxide (as well as other gases) in ocean water varies with depth. It tends to be more abundant at the surface. However, ocean currents ensure that some carbon dioxide is distributed to the depths. Here, the gas is in long-term storage.

Heat, too, is stored in the water. Oceans absorb vast quantities of heat. Warm water, such as that near the equator, is less dense than cold water. It floats on the surface and slowly moves northward and southward toward the poles. Meanwhile, in the polar regions, water is cooled. It sinks, then moves toward the equator. Without these currents that carry water back and forth between the equator and the poles, the oceans would be very different. At the equator, temperatures would be too high to support life. Near the poles, everything would be frozen solid.

Eventually, heat absorbed by the ocean is transferred to the atmosphere. Some heat passes directly to air molecules that are in direct contact with ocean waters. Some heat radiates from the ocean surface, mostly at night when there is the greatest difference between the water temperature and the air temperature.

4
HUMAN ACTIVITY AND CARBON DIOXIDE LEVELS

You can live for days without food or water. But stop breathing, and in several minutes you will be dead. The purpose of breathing is to get oxygen into the body and get wastes such as carbon dioxide out.

Breathing isn't the only human activity that produces carbon dioxide. The gas is a byproduct of many industrial processes, including the fermentation of sugars to produce alcohol, the decomposition of limestone to make quicklime and the manufacture of cement. But the main sources are the burning of fossil fuels and the destruction of forests.

Burning Fossil Fuels

The amount of carbon dioxide in the atmosphere has been rising ever since people began burning fossil fuels in large quantities. Fossil fuels are preserved forms of carbon. They are formed in the Earth from the remains of dead plants and animals. When the organisms died, some were buried and ended up under great pressure deep beneath the Earth's surface. The pressure changed them into coal, oil and natural gas. When these fuels are burned, the carbon that was stored in them combines with oxygen to form carbon dioxide.

Some fossil fuels are burned to produce heat. Large quantities are burned to produce electricity, which runs machines and appliances, heats and cools buildings, lights our rooms

Opposite page: Humans are a significant source of carbon dioxide. After we inhale air (oxygen) into our lungs, we release carbon dioxide as waste through exhalation.

and does many other jobs for us. And large quantities are used to operate vehicles: cars, trucks, motorcycles, buses, trains, planes, ships and so on.

The burning of fossil fuels releases about 5.6 billion tons of carbon dioxide into the air every year. This amount is expected to increase. Some scientists estimate that the number will jump to as much as 30 billion tons per year within the next few decades.

Industrial nations contribute about 75% of the release, or emission, of carbon dioxide from burning fossil fuels. In fact, carbon dioxide levels are typically higher over large industrial cities than elsewhere. In the cities, there is more burning of fossil fuels, more people who breathe out carbon dioxide, and fewer green plants to use up the carbon dioxide.

Destroying Forests

Forests are one of our most important defenses against global warming. They are like giant sponges, soaking up huge amounts of carbon dioxide. But throughout the world, people are destroying forests at an alarming rate.

Deforestation increases carbon dioxide levels in the atmosphere in two basic ways. When trees decay or are burned, they release the carbon they have absorbed over their entire lifetime. And without the forests, carbon dioxide that would have been absorbed for photosynthesis remains in the air.

Clearing Forests

People cut down trees for many reasons: to obtain fuel; to fill the demand for wood products; to create farms and grazing lands; and to expand towns and cities.

This is happening in all parts of the world. But the problem is particularly severe in tropical forests, such as the one in the Amazon River basin of South America. According to a report issued by the World Resources Institute in 1990, 40 to 50 million acres (16 to 20 million hectares) of tropical forests are being cleared each year. That's almost an acre and a half a second! Or to look at it another way, each year an area the size of the state of Washington is being stripped of trees. Brazil is

HEAT ISLANDS

Want to plant tomatoes? Consider moving to a city! Why? Because growing seasons are longer. In Chicago and Washington, D.C., for example, frost-free growing seasons are a month longer than in the surrounding rural areas.

Cities generate so much heat that their temperatures may be significantly higher than that of the surrounding countryside. One source of this heat is the burning of fossil fuels: There are many more vehicles, furnaces, factories and other fuel-using devices in a city than outside the city. There are more people, who give off body heat. And the buildings, roads and sidewalks absorb solar energy rather than reflect it.

This "heat island" effect can be found in cities all over the world. People and the environment pay for this heat. It is estimated that for every degree Fahrenheit generated within a heat island, 2% more energy is used just for additional air conditioning. Smog also increases as urban temperatures rise.

losing over 12.5 million acres of tropical forest a year; India, 3.7 million acres; Indonesia, 2.2 million acres.

Meteorologist Jagadish Shukla of the University of Maryland used a computer to predict the effects of deforestation along the Amazon River. He found that the loss of trees would cause rainfall in the area to decline by more than 26%, from the current 97 inches (2.5 meters) a year to about 72 inches (1.8 meters) a year. This would mean that the rain forest now found in the Amazon basin could not be replaced, for it wouldn't survive in the new, drier climate. Other environments would also be affected. The Amazon River empties huge amounts of fresh water into the Atlantic Ocean. As rainfall decreased, so would the amount of water carried to the Atlantic. This, in turn, would change the chemistry of the oceans, which would affect the plants and animals living there. As the chemistry and ecology of the oceans changed, there could be global effects on the climate.

Acid Rain

Another cause of deforestation is the burning of fossil fuels, particularly coal and oil. When these fuels are burned, sulfur dioxide and nitrogen oxides are produced as wastes. Sulfur dioxide comes primarily from the smokestacks of power plants, smelters and other industrial facilities. Nitrogen oxides come from smokestacks and from the exhausts of automobiles and other vehicles.

VALLEY OF DEATH

High in the Andean mountains of Peru lies the Huallaga Valley. Once it was covered with a dense, lush rain forest. By the late 1980s, however, much of the jungle was gone. People were destroying an estimated 3 acres (1.2 hectares) or more of forest every day. They were replacing the rich habitat with a new kind of forest—a forest of coca bushes. More than 250,000 acres (100,000 hectares) had been planted with coca bushes, whose leaves are the raw material for cocaine. The Huallaga had become the "Valley of Death."

The destruction of this rain forest has had many effects. Increased carbon dioxide in the atmosphere is an invisible effect. More obvious are the muddied rivers, loaded with sediments washed from the now-bare hillsides. Trees hold soil in place. As the soil is stripped away, the land's ability to support jungle plants—or even coca bushes—decreases, bringing the threat of desertification (the process of becoming arid land or desert). The rivers also carry deadly chemicals produced during the processing of the coca leaves. Marc Dourojeanni, a professor of forestry at Peru's National Agrarian University, calculated that in 1987, 15 million gallons (56.8 million liters) of kerosene, 8 million gallons (30 million liters) of sulfuric acid, 1.6 million gallons (6 million liters) of acetone and 1.6 million gallons (6 million liters) of toluene solvent were dumped into rivers and streams in the Upper Huallaga Valley.

And where has the wildlife gone? The jungles of Peru are home for a wonderful variety of animals. Spectacled bears, monkeys, jaguars, parrots, toucans, translucent-winged butterflies and other insects find shelter in the canopies of interlocking leaves and branches. As the jungles are destroyed to grow coca, the animals suffer, for without their environment they cannot survive.

Enormous amounts of these gases are produced. A single smokestack may produce as much as 500 tons of sulfur dioxide a day. All together, millions upon millions of tons of the gases are discharged into the atmosphere each year.

In the atmosphere, the gases combine with oxygen and moisture to form solutions of sulfuric acid and nitric acid. When rain falls, it carries the acids to the ground. We call this precipitation acid rain. The term actually refers to any precipitation that is acidic—not only rain but also snow, sleet, mist and fog. In addition, the acids can be deposited dry, as gases or as part of microscopic particles.

As the acids seep into the ground, they may change the chemistry of the soil. They may deplete the soil of calcium and magnesium, elements needed by plants for the formation of chlorophyll and wood. The acids also may cause the release of aluminum in the soil. Aluminum is poisonous and can kill the roots of trees. It also decreases the ability of trees to absorb any calcium and magnesium that may remain in the soil.

Some plants, particularly acid-loving plants such as blueberry bushes and mountain laurel, do not appear to be harmed by increasing acidity. Other plants are much more sensitive. They will die if the soil is too acidic.

Among the most threatened plants are coniferous, or cone-bearing, trees such as spruce and fir. In some places, large forests have been destroyed. One such place is Mount Mitchell in North Carolina—the highest mountain east of the Mississippi River. Until the early 1980s, a red spruce forest covered the top of Mount Mitchell. In less than a decade, the trees were dead. The landscape was dotted with bare trunks and branches—the skeletons of a recently thriving forest.

Often, the acids are carried great distances by winds. They are carried from one state to another, from one nation to another. For example, about half of the sulfur deposited in eastern Canada originates in the United States, particularly in the Ohio Valley area. Robert I. Bruck, a plant pathologist at North Carolina State University who studied the decline of trees on Mount Mitchell, was "90% certain" that polluted air from the Ohio and Tennessee valleys were the cause of the extensive damage on the mountain.

Ozone

Another chemical implicated in forest decline is ozone. Ozone is a form of oxygen that contains three atoms per molecule (O_3). On Earth, it is produced mainly by automobile and truck exhausts. Scientists have found that ozone slows tree growth. They have also shown that it speeds the aging of needles in some kinds of pine seedlings.

One place where ozone damage is visible is in the San Bernardino Mountains near Los Angeles. Here, ozone from the area's millions of cars have damaged and slowed growth in ponderosa pines. It has also made the trees more susceptible to insects and root diseases.

The World's Booming Population

As the world began the last decade of the 20th century, some 5.3 billion people populated its lands. Every day, the number grows: three more births every second, about a quarter of a million births every day. The United Nations Population Fund predicted that, if it continues to grow at the same rate, the world's population will reach 6.25 billion by the end of the 1990s—the equivalent of adding an extra China.

SEASONAL UPS AND DOWNS

The amount of atmospheric carbon dioxide varies with the seasons. Levels are lowest during the summer, when green plants are actively growing. During this time, plants take huge amounts of carbon dioxide out of the atmosphere for photosynthesis. In autumn, leaves fall to the ground and decay. This process releases carbon dioxide. The amount of atmospheric carbon dioxide rises.

In winter, many plants are dormant. Less carbon dioxide is absorbed, so that more of it remains in the atmosphere. In the Northern Hemisphere, the highest levels of carbon dioxide are found at the end of winter, as spring begins. By late September or early October, they have fallen to their lowest levels.

There is some evidence that swings from one extreme to the other are getting wider. One possible explanation: Increased carbon dioxide from the burning of fossil fuels may stimulate trees to produce more leaves.

To remain alive, each person must get energy from food. In the process, carbon dioxide is produced and exhaled into the environment. A great amount of additional carbon dioxide is produced by farm machinery that gathers the food, trucks and other vehicles that transport the food, supermarkets that sell the food and cars used by people to travel to and from the supermarkets. More people also means more houses, schools, factories, hospitals and other buildings to be heated in winter and cooled in summer. It means more machines, more appliances and so on.

Most of the population growth is occurring in developing countries. This means greater numbers of poor and hungry people putting increased pressure on already stressed lands, forests and water supplies.

"These increasing numbers are eating away at the earth itself," wrote Nafis Sadik, executive director of the U.N. Population Fund. "The combination of fast population growth in poor countries has begun to make permanent changes to the environment. During the 1990s these changes will reach critical levels. They include continued urban growth; degradation of land and water resources; massive deforestation; and buildup of greenhouse gases. Many of these changes are now inevitable because they were not foreseen early enough, or because action was not taken to forestall them. Our options in the present generation are narrow because of the decisions of our predecessors. Our range of choice, as individuals or as nations, is narrower and the choices are harder."

Sadik is among the many people who stress the need to slow population growth. In industrialized nations, the birth rate now averages 1.9 children per woman. This is below the replacement level—that is, the level at which births equal deaths and the population remains constant (i.e., two children replace two parents). In developing nations, however, the birth rate averages 3.9. This is significantly higher than the replacement level, which means populations are growing rapidly in those nations.

According to the latest U.N. projections, the world is now on course for a population close to 11 billion by the end of the

The Problems

As global warming intensifies, fertile farmland will dry up and become barren.

BURNING FOSSIL FUELS pours huge amounts of carbon dioxide and other heat-trapping gases into the atmosphere. Fossil fuels are burned to operate cars and other vehicles, to heat buildings and to produce electricity. Every year, the burning of these fuels releases about 5.6 billion tons of carbon dioxide into the air—an amount that is expected to increase. The increasing concentration of carbon dioxide in the atmosphere threatens the delicate balance between the amount of solar energy reaching Earth and the heat radiating outward from Earth and its atmosphere. The carbon dioxide allows the solar energy to pass through the atmosphere, but it prevents heat given off by Earth from escaping into space. As more and more heat is given off, the atmosphere becomes warmer and warmer. This process is called the greenhouse effect.

Left: Daily rush hour traffic clogs the San Diego Freeway in Los Angeles, California. *Above:* Smokestacks spew pollutants at a steel plant in Geneva, Utah.

THE COMBINED HEAT-TRAPPING EFFECT of chlorofluorocarbons (CFCs), methane and nitrous oxide equals or is greater than that of carbon dioxide. CFCs are used as aerosol propellants, refrigerants, cleaning solvents and raw materials for making plastic foam. Livestock, burning vegetation and decomposition are major sources of methane. Nitrous oxide—used as an anesthetic in some dental and surgical procedures—comes primarily from nitrogen-based fertilizers, deforestation and the burning of vegetation and fossil fuels.

Above: Many aerosol sprays commonly use chlorofluorocarbons (CFCs) as propellants. *Right*: Digestive gas from livestock is a major source of methane in the atmosphere. *Far right*: Nitrous oxide—or "laughing gas"— is often used in many dental procedures.

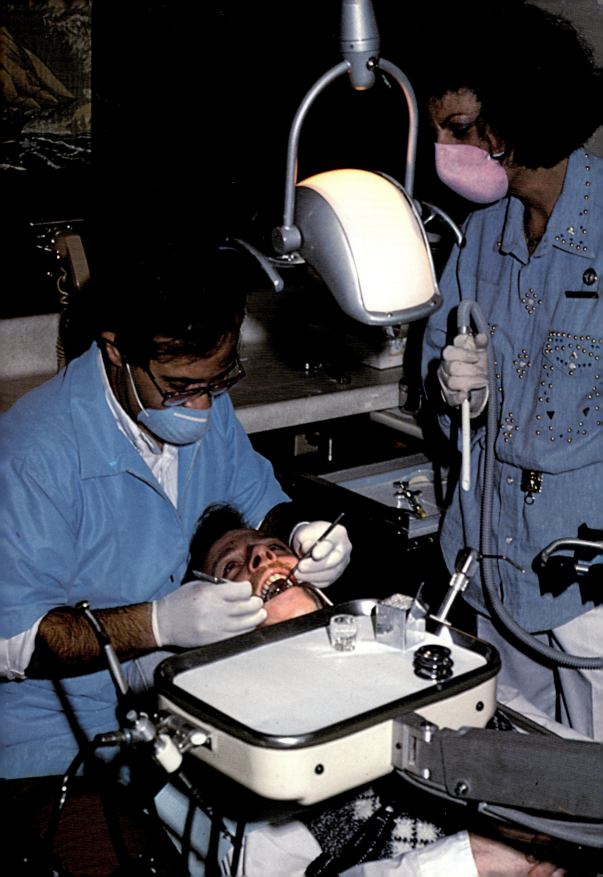

An area in Everglades National Park, Florida, dries slowly in the sun.

As GLOBAL TEMPERATURES INCREASE there will be a rise in the average water level of the oceans. Gradually, low-lying coastal areas will be inundated. This will result in the loss of crucial wetlands located along seacoasts. Rising seas, coupled with changing climate and weather patterns, will also threaten seaside communities with frequent flooding and damage from increasingly violent storms.

Above: A fierce typhoon batters the coast of Moorea, one of the Society Islands in the South Pacific.

The lure of sun worship has lessened in recent years, due to warnings of increasing dangers.

SOME AIR POLLUTANTS are creating an additional atmospheric problem: they are destroying the ozone layer, a concentration of ozone in the stratosphere that protects Earth from harmful ultraviolet radiation. As the ozone layer thins and the amount of ultraviolet radiation reaching Earth increases, there will be more and more cases of skin cancer.

next century. But, points out Sadik, "if fertility reductions continue to be slower than projected . . . the world could be headed toward an eventual total of up to 14 billion people."

Measuring the Danger

Carbon dioxide levels have been rising steadily since the beginning of the industrial revolution. This revolution, which began in England about 1760, marked the transformation of traditional, mainly agricultural, societies into modern societies. Manufacturing moved from homes to factories. Machines began to do work previously done by human hands—machines powered in large part by fossil fuels. As the revolution spread and the number of factories and machines grew, the use of fossil fuels accelerated.

In 1958, Charles D. Keeling, an atmospheric scientist at Scripps Institution of Oceanography, set up a laboratory atop Mauna Loa. This high volcano on the island of Hawaii is far away from sources of industrial pollution. This makes Mauna Loa an ideal place to monitor changes in the atmosphere. Keeling found that the concentration of carbon dioxide was 315 parts per million. Over the years, a continuously operated infrared gas analyzer has continued to take measurements—except for rare occasions when work is interrupted by the eruption of the smoldering volcano!

The concentration of carbon dioxide in the air over Mauna Loa has steadily grown. It reached 340 parts per million in the early 1980s and almost 360 parts per million by 1990. These figures have been confirmed by measurements taken in other parts of the world, from Alaska all the way to the South Pole.

Scientists have found that the concentration of carbon dioxide in air trapped in glacial ice a century ago was about 280 parts per million. Thus, in the last 100 years, carbon dioxide concentration has increased more than 25%. What is particularly worrisome is the rate at which this increase has occurred. If the present rate of increase continues, the carbon dioxide concentration could reach as much as 600 parts per million by the year 2040! This would cause a substantial increase in the temperature on the surface of our planet.

5
Heat Traps

Carbon dioxide isn't the only gas that traps heat in the atmosphere. So do more than 30 other gases. Most of these gases are byproducts of human activities, produced by many different types of processes—everything from growing rice to cleaning computer chips.

Each of these gases is emitted in much smaller quantities than carbon dioxide. Like carbon dioxide, the concentration of these heat traps is growing, and growing at an increasing rate. By 1990, these gases had reached levels at which their combined heat-trapping effect was actually greater than that of carbon dioxide. Many experts believe that over the next 50 years their effect will continue to outpace that of carbon dioxide. One reason is that they are far more efficient than carbon dioxide at absorbing infrared radiation, the type of radiation that ordinarily carries the Earth's excess heat into space. One molecule of some chlorofluorocarbons can absorb more heat than 10,000 molecules of carbon dioxide!

Also, carbon dioxide absorbs only certain wavelengths of infrared radiation. The trace gases absorb other, additional wavelengths. Among the gases causing the most concern are nitrous oxide, methane and chlorofluorocarbons.

Laughing Gas

Nitrous oxide is a colorless gas with a sweet taste and sweet odor. One of its uses is as an anesthetic in brief procedures such as minor surgery and dentistry. When enough nitrous

Opposite page: Gases other than carbon dioxide—such as methane—trap heat in the atmosphere. Much of the methane in our atmosphere has come from the burning of vegetation and forests.

oxide is inhaled it causes unconsciousness. But in lesser amounts or before consciousness is lost, the person experiences a feeling of cheerfulness bordering on mild hysteria. Because of this reaction, nitrous oxide acquired the name "laughing gas."

The major source of nitrous oxide in the atmosphere is nitrogen-based fertilizers. Other important sources are deforestation, the burning of plants and the burning of fossil fuels.

Nitrous oxide (N_2O) is responsible for about 6% of the human contributions to greenhouse warming. It has increased in concentration by 5% to 10% over the past 200 years. Currently, it is increasing at a rate of 0.25% per year.

Cow Gas

Methane (CH_4) makes up 18% of human contributions to the greenhouse effect. Its concentration in the atmosphere has doubled in the past 300 years, from 650 to 1,700 parts per billion in volume. Currently, it is increasing at a rate of 1% a year. An estimated 425 to 675 tons are added to the atmosphere each year.

Natural Sources

Approximately 40% of atmospheric methane comes from natural sources. Methane is produced during respiration in anaerobic places—that is, in places where oxygen is not available. Such places include wet soils in swamps, marshes, bogs, lakes and oceans. They also include the flooded fields, called paddies, in which rice is grown. In these anaerobic places, bacteria that decompose animal and vegetable matter produce methane as a waste product.

Huge amounts of methane produced by bacterial respiration are stored at the bottom of the ocean and in frozen tundra. Global warming may cause the ocean sediments and tundra to release this methane into the atmosphere.

Human Sources

Human activities are believed to account for approximately 60% of the methane emitted each year. The major source is

HARBINGERS OF GLOBAL CHANGE

"I have seen nothing in the way of twilight effect so strange as that of Monday evening, the 6th, when about 10 P.M. a sea of luminous silvery white cloud lay above a belt of ordinary clear twilight sky, which was rather low in tone and colour. These clouds were wave-like in form, and evidently at a great elevation, and though they must have received their light from the sun, it was not easy to think so, as upon the dark sky they looked brighter and paler than clouds under a full moon. A friend who was with me aptly compared the light on these clouds to that which shines from white phosphor paint."

Robert C. Leslie wrote these words to *Nature* magazine in July 1885. The clouds he described—now called noctilucent clouds—had not been observed before that year. But in the succeeding years they have become increasingly common. Why?

"Noctilucent clouds represent in our era a kind of a sentinel—a sign in the sky telling us we are doing things to our planet," says meteorologist John J. Olivero of Penn State University.

These clouds are the highest, coldest clouds on Earth. They appear only in summer, forming in the stratosphere, most commonly in polar latitudes. At first, scientists assumed they were a natural phenomenon. But today it is known that water vapor in air doesn't reach the heights where noctilucent clouds form. It precipitates or is frozen before reaching the stratosphere.

Today, scientists believe noctilucent clouds result from increasing levels of methane gas in the upper atmosphere. Unlike water vapor, methane rises into the stratosphere. There it breaks down and releases hydrogen. The hydrogen combines with a hydroxyl radical (an atom of hydrogen attached to an atom of oxygen) to form water. On the average, two water molecules are produced from every methane molecule. The more methane reaching the stratosphere, the greater the amount of water that forms.

Because of the very low temperatures, the water forms tiny ice crystals that scatter sunlight. And since they are so high in the sky, they are illuminated long after the Earth's surface has been darkened by nightfall.

Olivero suggests that rising carbon dioxide levels may warm the stratosphere, thus altering conditions under which noctilucent clouds form. "I can foresee a time," he says, "in 10 or 100 years, when there will no longer be noctilucent clouds."

the cultivation of rice, which accounts for an estimated 20% of annual methane emissions. Raising livestock accounts for about 15%. Cattle, sheep, goats and other cud-chewing animals give off methane—in burps and flatulence—as they digest food. The methane is made by bacteria that live in the animals' digestive tract and aid in the digestion of hay and other plant matter. Additional methane is released from the wastes of the livestock.

Burning vegetation contributes 10% of the methane emissions. Sometimes, this is a natural phenomenon, as fire sweeps through a forest or across a prairie. Often, however, the fires are started by people, as a quick way to clear land for cultivation. Chopping down forests also adds to methane levels as plants decay. Termites flourish in some deforested areas, feeding on the remains of trees. Like cattle, their digestive tracts contain methane-producing bacteria that help break down food.

Municipal landfills emit methane as bacteria break down food scraps, grass cuttings and other organic garbage. Finally, methane is the major constituent of natural gas. A certain amount of methane is released into the air as leakage from wells and pipelines during the recovery and distribution of the fuel. Additional amounts are released during coal mining, oil drilling and petroleum refining.

This gas is potent but short-lived. Methane is 20 to 30 times more potent than carbon dioxide in absorbing heat radiated from the Earth's surface. Fortunately, its lifetime in the atmosphere is relatively short. It exists only about 10 years before being destroyed through reactions with other substances in the atmosphere. In comparison, other greenhouse gases have atmospheric lifetimes of 100 years or more.

Therefore, stabilizing or decreasing methane levels in the atmosphere would be comparatively easy to accomplish. Scientists estimate that a reduction of 10% to 20% in methane emissions would stabilize methane concentrations in the atmosphere. On the other hand, they believe that it would take a 50% to 80% reduction to stabilize carbon dioxide levels and almost a 100% reduction to stabilize chlorofluorocarbon levels in the atmosphere.

Refrigerator Gas

In 1928, Thomas Widgley Jr., a chemist working at the Frigidaire Division of General Motors, invented a new refrigerant. Unlike ammonia and other refrigerants used at the time, it was a very stable compound. It did not react easily with other chemicals. This made it nontoxic, nonflammable and noncorrosive. In other words, a great improvement over existing refrigerants.

Widgley's new chemical was named Freon. It was the first chlorofluorocarbon (CFC)—an entirely new compound containing chlorine, fluorine and carbon. Many other CFCs were developed in the following years. And new uses were found for the chemicals. Today, in addition to being used as coolants in refrigerators and air conditioners, CFCs are used as aerosol propellants in spray cans, medical sterilizers, cleaning solvents for electronic components and raw materials for

RADICALS IN THE ATMOSPHERE

Unlike CFCs, most polluting gases undergo chemical changes in the lower atmosphere. They react with hydroxyl radicals and are changed into water-soluble substances—that is, substances that can be dissolved in water. They can then be removed from the air by precipitation.

A radical is a fragment of a molecule that maintains its identity when chemical changes affect the rest of the molecule. The hydroxyl radical (OH) consists of an atom of oxygen and an atom of hydrogen. Usually, it is part of a larger molecule, such as water (H_2O) or baking soda ($NaHCO_3$). If the large molecule is split apart, the hydroxyl radical continues to exist as a unit rather than breaking up into separate atoms of oxygen and hydrogen. Not for long, however—hydroxyl radicals exist but a fraction of a second before they react with some other chemical in the atmosphere.

At any moment, there are comparatively few free hydroxyl radicals. Their concentration in the atmosphere is less than .00001 part per billion. Even in such low concentrations, they play an important role. They help clean the atmosphere. If it weren't for their "detergent" abilities, much of the methane, sulfur dioxide, carbon monoxide and other pollutants released into the air over the ages would still be there.

Are all the pollutants we're dumping into the atmosphere causing a decline in the amount of hydroxyl radicals? If so, what will happen to the quality of the lower atmosphere containing air we breathe?

---

making plastic foam objects such as coffee cups. Approximately 2.2 billion pounds (1 billion kilograms) of CFCs are produced annually. About one-third of this amount is used in the United States, largely as refrigerants.

Before companies started manufacturing CFCs in the 1930s, there were no CFCs in the atmosphere. Now, CFCs are estimated to account for 14% of global warming. One reason for this is that CFCs are very powerful greenhouse gases. A CFC molecule is 10,000 times more efficient than a carbon dioxide molecule at trapping heat.

But its heat-trapping ability is only part of why CFCs are so dangerous. These chemicals are not destroyed or removed in the lower atmosphere. Instead, they slowly drift into the stratosphere. High above the Earth, they create a second problem: They destroy ozone. This subject is discussed in the next chapter.

When they were developed, CFCs seemed wonderful. Their qualities were praised. Today, we know much more about CFCs. As a result, we view them very differently. The problems they are causing support Cornell University astronomer Carl Sagan's comment on many of the environmental threats that confront us—"The lesson is clear: we are not always smart or wise enough to foresee the consequences of our actions."

6

A Hole in the Sky

Antarctica is the most desolate place on Earth. Located at the South Pole, this continent lies buried beneath a vast ice sheet that holds 70% of the world's fresh water. No native people live there. Nor do many plants and animals.

The sparseness of life on ice-covered land contrasts greatly with the ecosystem of the surrounding seas. Seals, whales, giant squids, fish, penguins and seabirds frequent these waters, which are rich in microscopic organisms that form the basis of the ecosystem's food chain.

Through the years, people's activities have often threatened the organisms in this ecosystem. Overhunting has decimated whale populations. Oil pollution has killed seabirds. Global warming threatens temperature changes that could doom some species. But these threats may pale in significance when compared with a new threat discovered in the 1980s: There is a "hole" in the sky over Antarctica. Chemicals from human activities have caused a dramatic thinning of the ozone layer in the atmosphere over Antarctica. As a result, increased levels of harmful radiation are reaching the land and the surrounding seas.

A Delayed Discovery

Preconceptions are dangerous. In the scientific community they can cloud thinking, preventing people from seeing

Opposite page: Chemicals from human activities have caused a serious deterioration of the Earth's ozone layer, increasing the level of harmful radiation that reaches land from the sun.

> ### THE FOUR SEASONS
>
> Spring, summer, fall, winter: Most parts of the world experience these four seasons, with their varying temperatures, weather conditions and lengths of days. The seasons change because the Earth's axis is tilted with regard to its orbit. While one pole is tilted toward the sun, the other pole is tilted away from the sun.
>
> July is the middle of summer in the Northern Hemisphere. People spend long, sunny days at picnics, beaches and ballparks. But in Antarctica, it is winter. The continent lies in total darkness. No sunlight reaches Antarctica during this time because the South Pole is tilted away from the sun. Six months later, the Earth is halfway around its orbit, on the opposite side of the sun. In January, it is summer in the Southern Hemisphere—and winter in the Northern Hemisphere.

THE SEASONS

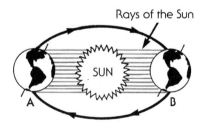

A Summer in Northern Hemisphere
   Winter in Southern Hemisphere

B Winter in Northern Hemisphere
   Summer in Southern Hemisphere

things that they do not expect. Such was the case with the hole in the ozone layer. For several years, the hole went unnoticed or unrecognized by the scientists who operated the international network of ozone-monitoring stations. When it was finally noticed, scientists doubted its existence. Instead, they questioned the accuracy of their instruments.

The British Antarctic Survey, which has a research station at Halley Bay in Antarctica, has used spectrophotometers to measure ozone in the atmosphere there ever since 1957. In 1976, the scientists detected a 10% drop in ozone levels during the Antarctic spring (September, October and November). They didn't attach much significance to this because ozone concentrations in Antarctica often fluctuate from season to season, even from day to night.

In the spring of 1977, another drop in ozone levels was recorded. None was recorded in 1978, but declines were again recorded in succeeding years. Suspecting that their spectrophotometer was inaccurate, the scientists waited for a new, carefully calibrated instrument to be sent from England. In the spring of 1983, when both spectrophotometers registered record-low levels, the scientists realized that something significant was happening. But no one else was reporting anything unusual.

The U.S. National Aeronautics and Space Administration (NASA) had an ozone mapper spectrometer aboard the Nimbus 7 weather satellite, which had been passing over Antarctica 14 times a day since 1978. It wasn't until 1984 that a NASA scientist, studying the satellite readings, saw that the ozone levels over Antarctica appeared to have dropped 50% during the spring of 1983. But a ground-based spectrophotometer at the U.S. Amundsen-Scott base recorded normal concentrations. American scientists concluded that the spectrometer aboard Nimbus 7 was malfunctioning. But it was the ground-based instrument that was incorrect.

In the spring of 1984, British scientists again recorded a large drop in ozone over Halley Bay. Another ground station, a thousand miles to the north, also recorded the change. In 1985, the British Antarctic Survey published its data, showing that a 40% loss in total ozone had occurred since the 1960s over Halley Bay during September, October and early November.

American and Japanese scientists soon confirmed that the phenomenon was indeed real. And in every year since, the ozone hole has recurred during the spring months.

In 1988, scientists reported that atmospheric ozone levels also had declined over most other parts of the world, though not as severely as over Antarctica. For example, between 30 degrees and 60 degrees North latitude—an area that includes most of the United States, Canada, Europe, the Soviet Union, China and Japan—concentrations had decreased as much as 3% between 1969 and 1986.

What Is Ozone?

Unlike ordinary oxygen, which has two atoms per molecule (O_2), ozone has three atoms per molecule (O_3). The difference of one atom is a difference of life and death. Plants and animals must breathe oxygen to live. But were they to breathe more than a trace of ozone, they would die, for ozone is poisonous even in small concentrations.

Ozone comprises only a tiny fraction of the atmosphere. If all of it were compressed near the Earth's surface at normal temperature and pressure, it would form a layer only 0.12 inch (3 millimeters) thick. Its distribution through the atmosphere is not uniform, however. Most ozone is found in the stratosphere, the layer 10 to 30 miles (17 to 50 kilometers) above the Earth's surface.

Also present in this high-altitude layer is atomic oxygen (O)—oxygen in the form of single atoms instead of molecules. The quantities of atomic oxygen (O), ordinary oxygen (O_2) and ozone (O_3) fluctuate as molecules break apart and reform in response to solar radiation and other influences. Until comparatively recent years, however, an equilibrium existed. The concentration of each form of oxygen remained relatively constant.

HOW OZONE IS DESTROYED

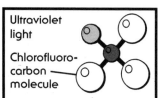

1. In the upper atmosphere a chlorine atom is separated from a chlorofluorocarbon molecule through the action of ultraviolet light.

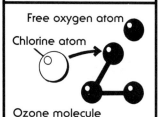

2. The chlorine atom causes a molecule of ozone to break apart.

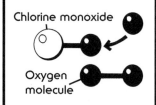

3. This causes the formation of a molecule of oxygen and a molecule of chlorine monoxide.

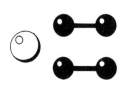

4. A free oxygen molecule breaks up the newly formed chlorine monoxide molecule. This frees the chlorine atom to repeat the sequence.

How Ozone Is Formed—and Destroyed

The radiant energy emitted by the sun has many forms. The most familiar form is visible light, or white light, which is a mixture of light of all colors. At either end of this visible spectrum are various forms of invisible radiation. One of these is ultraviolet radiation.

At ground level, ultraviolet light is harmful to living things. Fortunately, only a very small portion of the sun's ultraviolet radiation reaches the Earth's surface. Most is absorbed in the stratosphere. There, it plays critical roles in the formation and destruction of ozone.

When ultraviolet radiation is absorbed by a molecule of ordinary oxygen, it breaks the bond that holds together the two oxygen atoms, in a reaction called dissociation. This can be represented by an equation:

$$O_2 + UV \rightarrow O + O$$

When each of the single oxygen atoms combines with a molecule of ordinary oxygen, a molecule of ozone is formed:

$$O + O_2 \rightarrow O_3$$

This step requires the presence of a catalyst, a substance that speeds up a reaction. Usually, nitrogen acts as the catalyst in the formation of ozone, but other atmospheric substances could also do so.

The bonds holding together the oxygen atoms in the ozone molecule are not as strong as those in an oxygen molecule. As a result, ozone breaks apart comparatively easily. This splitting of the ozone molecule by ultraviolet radiation can be shown as:

$$O_3 + UV \rightarrow O + O_2$$

Ozone also can be destroyed by a number of gases, including nitric oxide (NO). First, the nitric oxide breaks down the ozone, forming nitrogen dioxide (NO_2) and ordinary oxygen. Then, the nitrogen dioxide reacts with atomic oxygen, returning nitric oxide to the atmosphere. This "recycling" of nitric oxide means that small amounts of the substance can remove large quantities of ozone. The following equations show what happens when nitric oxide reacts with ozone:

$$NO + O_3 \rightarrow NO_2 + O_2$$
$$NO_2 + O \rightarrow NO + O_2$$

Airplane exhausts and the use of nitrogen fertilizers have increased the amounts of nitric oxide and nitrogen dioxide in the atmosphere, thereby increasing the rate of ozone breakdown. But the stratospheric ozone appears to be much more threatened by another human activity: the release of chlorofluorocarbons (CFCs). These gases are extremely stable in the lower atmosphere. In the stratosphere, however, they are dissociated by ultraviolet radiation. This releases chlorine atoms (Cl), which react with ozone. Chlorine monoxide (ClO) and oxygen (O_2) are formed. But the chlorine monoxide is soon split by ultraviolet radiation:

$$Cl + O_3 \rightarrow ClO + O_2$$
$$ClO + UV \rightarrow Cl + O$$

Here again, a destroyer of ozone is recycled. A chlorine atom may stay in the stratosphere for years before it is carried back into the lower atmosphere and washed out in rainwater. During the time it is in the stratosphere, it can take part in this reaction over and over again. A single chlorine atom may be able to destroy as many as 100,000 ozone molecules!

Increase the amount of chlorine, and the destruction of ozone jumps dramatically. Scientists estimate that before 1900 the level of chlorine in the stratosphere was about 0.6 parts per billion. Today, the chlorine level is about 3.5 parts per billion, and increasing by more than 1.0 part per billion per decade.

In 1987, high levels of chlorine were found in the Antarctic atmosphere. This strongly supports the theory that CFCs are a key factor in the destruction of atmospheric ozone. In fact, some researchers estimated that about 80% of the ozone loss over Antarctica in 1987 could be attributed to chlorine.

The future promises equal or greater losses. Even if people were to immediately stop all use of CFCs, the chlorine level

OZONE AND SMOG

Although ozone is beneficial high in the atmosphere, it is a pollutant at ground level. Ozone is the major component of smog, forming when sunlight causes a reaction between nitrogen oxides and volatile organic compounds. Nitrogen oxides come mainly from the burning of fossil fuels. The principal sources of volatile organic compounds are automobiles, factories and evaporating paints and dry cleaning solvents. The hotter the temperature, the greater the formation of ozone, in part because evaporation of chemicals speeds up in the heat.

In summer, stagnant air masses build up over urban centers such as Los Angeles and Mexico City. During this time, ozone levels can be dangerously high. Ozone causes breathing problems, particularly among young children, the elderly and people with asthma and other respiratory ailments. It can also cause chest pains and coughing in joggers and other people who exercise strenuously. In addition, research with animals indicates that long-term exposure to high ozone levels may cause permanent damage to the lungs.

SUN AND SHADOW

Many studies have confirmed the relationship between sunlight and skin cancer. One particularly telling project compared the incidence of skin cancer in male drivers in the United States and Great Britain.

In the United States, drivers sit on the left side of the car. They expose the left side of the body to sunlight entering the side windows while keeping the right side of the body in the shadows. In Great Britain the reverse is true. Drivers sit next to the right-hand windows and expose the right side of the body to sunlight.

The result? In the United States, male drivers typically develop skin cancer on the left arm and the left side of the face. In Britain, drivers are more likely to get skin cancer on their right arm and right side of the face.

in the stratosphere would continue to rise for another decade or so because large quantities of CFCs are already in the lower atmosphere. It takes seven to ten years for CFCs to rise through the lower atmosphere and reach the stratosphere. Even without further releases of CFCs into the lower atmosphere, their level in the stratosphere is expected to double.

Consequences of Ozone Loss

As the ozone layer thins, increased amounts of ultraviolet radiation reach the Earth's surface, threatening the health of humans, animals and plants.

"As ozone decreases, you will get sunburns faster and worse," said Dr. John Hoffman, a global change specialist with the U.S. Environmental Protection Agency (EPA). Even more worrisome is the expected rise in the incidence of skin cancer. Skin cancer already is the most common kind of cancer in the United States, the Soviet Union and most northern European countries. Upwards of 500,000 new cases occur annually just in the United States. Most cases are treatable. But some 8,000 Americans die from the disease each year, often because they did not heed early warning signs and obtain treatment.

The chief culprit is excessive exposure to sunlight, particularly to a type of ultraviolet radiation called UV-B. As the amount of UV-B increases, so will the number of skin cancers. Every 1% increase in UV-B is expected to result in a 2% increase in skin cancers. The EPA has estimated that in the United States alone there will be more than 155 million additional cases of skin cancer and 3.2 million additional cancer deaths over the next century if ozone destruction continues at its current pace.

An increase in the incidence of eye cataracts is also expected. A cataract is the clouding of the lens, a normally transparent portion of the eye. In severe cases, the clouding can block all vision, causing blindness. Some cataracts are caused by injury, disease or chemical changes in the eye associated with aging. But many of them result from exposure to ultraviolet light. The only way to treat cataracts is to remove the clouded lens. The patient must either use special eyeglasses or contact lenses to focus the light entering the eye, or must have artificial lenses surgically implanted.

Ultraviolet radiation also harms the human immune system, the body's disease-fighting mechanism. Immunologists worry that increased levels of this radiation might change relatively minor infectious diseases into killers. It might also encourage the resurgence of such scourges as tuberculosis and leprosy. Plants and animals could be affected, too.

Of even greater concern than these human health problems, however, are the possible effects of increased ultraviolet radiation on ecosystems. Humans can shield themselves from radiation—by wearing protective clothing and sunglasses. But plants and animals have no protective mechanisms. Can they adapt to increasing levels of radiation?

In an experiment on soybeans, Dr. Alan F. Teramura of the University of Maryland found that an increase in radiation resulted in a decrease in photosynthesis, or food-making. By increasing radiation equivalent to that which would result from a 25% loss of ozone, Teramura caused a 20% to 25% drop in the yield of beans. If all crops suffered similar decreased yields, starvation in many parts of the world would result.

There is already evidence that photosynthesis declines in Antarctic waters when the ozone hole is in existence. The food-makers in these waters are phytoplankton. These microscopic algae form the basis for all the food chains in the Antarctic ecosystem. Without phytoplankton and the tiny animals that feed on them, there would be no food for penguins, seals, whales and the other large animals that live there. It is not yet known how big the decline in Antarctic photosynthesis is, nor what this portends for the animals in the ecosystem. But in a worst-case scenario, it could mean the extinction of many species.

The ozone hole over Antarctica is huge—as large as North America! And the loss of ozone elsewhere is occurring faster than ever before. In mid-1990, Ivar S. A. Isaksen of Norway's Institute of Geophysics reported that ozone levels over the middle latitudes of Europe and North America had fallen 10% since 1967—a significantly greater drop than had been reported even a year earlier.

7
PREDICTING THE FUTURE

"We should all be concerned about the future because we will have to spend the rest of our lives there." The American engineer and inventor Charles F. Kettering wrote these words in 1949. He might have added that our children and grandchildren will have to spend their lives there. What does that future hold? Will the Earth get warmer and warmer?

To answer this question, it is necessary to look at the past and the present. What changes have there been in temperature and atmospheric gas concentrations? What changes have taken place in populations and in people's activities? What is happening now? What trends are occurring and are these trends expected to continue?

Both direct and indirect evidence are important. Direct evidence is evidence you can see, touch or measure. For example, a thermometer reading is direct evidence of today's temperature. Indirect evidence cannot actually be seen, touched or measured. For example, based on studies of how matter behaves, scientists assumed the existence of atoms long before atoms were ever seen.

Cores of Ice

One type of direct evidence of changes in carbon dioxide levels comes from the thick ice sheets covering Greenland

Opposite page: Satellites that orbit the Earth have proven to be useful tools for measuring global temperatures.

and Antarctica. As snow fell onto the ice sheets and turned to ice, tiny air bubbles were trapped in the ice. Some of this air has been trapped in the ice sheets for tens of thousands of years. By analyzing air trapped at different times, scientists can learn how carbon dioxide levels have changed through the years.

A hollow drill is used to remove a long core of ice from the ice sheet. The upper part of the core is the newest ice. The deepest part is the oldest ice.

The most extensive study of air bubbles was carried out by a team at the Laboratory of Glaciology and Geophysics of the Environment in southern France. They examined more than 6,560 feet (2,000 meters) of ice core drilled by a joint French-Soviet team at Vostoc Station in Antarctica—a core of ice formed over a period of 160,000 years. During this time, warm periods alternated with cold periods called ice ages. The last ice age came to an end only about 10,000 years ago.

The scientists found that the carbon dioxide level remained relatively constant from 10,000 years ago until about 100 years ago, at approximately 260 parts per million. Then the level rose to its current level of 350 parts per million.

The level of methane changed, too. Until about 300 years ago, methane made up about 650 parts per billion. Then the level soared, reaching about 1,700 parts per billion today.

Equally important, as the levels of carbon dioxide and methane changed, so did the average temperature. As concentrations of the gases increased, so did the temperature. As the concentrations fell, so did the temperature. Did the changes in gas concentrations cause the temperature changes? Perhaps in some cases they did. That certainly appears to be the case during the past 130 years. But other factors are believed to have been involved during other periods.

Regardless of the cause, however, there is a correlation between increased levels of the gases and changes in temperature. "It is irresponsible to assume that after moving in tandem with carbon dioxide for 160,000 years, temperatures will not be affected by those dramatic increases [in recent and anticipated carbon dioxide levels]," commented U.S. Senator Albert Gore Jr.

Temperature Records

Another example of evidence comes from studying temperature readings over the past century. There are thousands of small weather stations around the world that routinely measure temperature. Two groups have used such historical information to construct records of global average surface temperatures.

A team led by Philip D. Jones at the Climatic Research Unit of the University of East Anglia in Great Britain found that global temperatures have risen an average of about 0.8° F (0.5° C) since 1900. James E. Hansen and his coworkers at NASA's Goddard Institute for Space Studies found a rise of 1.3° F (0.7° C).

In keeping with the trend, the 1980s was the warmest decade on record. Topping the temperature charts was 1988—the warmest year in the past century. Jones's group found that the worldwide average temperature for 1988 was 0.612° F (0.34° C) above the long-term average for the period 1950–79. The second hottest year of the century was 1987, followed by 1983, 1981, 1980 and 1989.

There are certain disadvantages with using surface records to estimate global atmospheric temperatures. Thermometers are not distributed evenly over the surface of the Earth. Land-based weather stations tend to be concentrated in developed areas, including urban areas where the heat-island effect can skew results. Temperatures at large areas of the ocean—which covers 70% of the Earth's surface—are not yet measured.

Jones is among those who have tried to take such factors into account. He reported that even though an urban bias in the data may be responsible for present records that show global warming over the past century, it does not account for the entire rise in temperature.

A more accurate method for measuring global temperatures may be the use of satellites in orbit around the Earth. The first data on global temperatures from satellites was reported in 1990 by Roy W. Spencer of the Marshall Space Flight Center and John R. Christy of the University of Alabama. They analyzed data collected between 1979 and 1988 by instruments aboard the TIROS-N series of weather

---

EL NIÑO AND LA NIÑA

Many natural phenomena cause considerable fluctuations in climate and temperature. Among them are cyclical changes in the surface waters of the tropical Pacific. These changes are known as El Niño (Spanish for "the boy") and La Niña ("the girl").

El Niño involves a major warming of the Pacific Ocean waters. The warm waters flow toward South America, displacing the cold Humboldt Current. As a result, millions of fish die, ruining Peru's fishing industry. Unusually heavy rains fall in Peru and nearby Ecuador—and sometimes as far north as California. Meanwhile, at the other end of the Pacific, in Australia and Indonesia, there is severe drought. El Niños occur roughly every three to seven years. Each lasts from 12 to 18 months.

The opposite of El Niño is La Niña. This recently recognized phenomenon involves a drop of temperature in the equatorial Pacific. Australia and Indonesia experience heavy rains while areas such as Peru and western Mexico tend to dry out.

What causes El Niño and La Niña? For some reason, there is an abnormal transfer of heat between the ocean and the atmosphere. But scientists have yet to determine what causes this heat transfer.

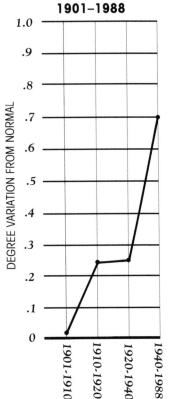

LARGEST ANNUAL AVERAGE TEMPERATURE VARIATION ABOVE NORMAL 1901–1988

satellites. The instruments, called passive microwave radiometers, measure microwave radiation caused by heating of the first 6 miles (9.6 kilometers) of atmosphere above the Earth's surface.

Spencer and Christy found large fluctuations in global temperatures. They detected "no obvious trend for the 10-year period." It was generally agreed that 10 years is too short a period to determine warming trends. It will take at least another decade of measurements to learn if the satellites are finding evidence of global warming.

Global Circulation Models

To obtain a general idea of what might be in store for the future, scientists use highly complex computer programs called climate models. The programs contain numerous mathematical equations that represent the physical processes in the atmosphere. Massive amounts of data are plugged into the programs—numbers on temperature, pressure and other factors at different points in the atmosphere—and analyzed using supercomputers.

The greater the number of atmospheric points covered, the more accurate the model. Models of small areas, such as the United States, are quite accurate and are very useful in weather forecasting. But to predict worldwide trends, models of larger areas, such as the Northern Hemisphere or the entire planet, are necessary. These are called global circulation models, or GCMs.

Scientists also use computer models to study economic trends. Such models can, for example, estimate how much fossil fuel will be burned in the coming years. This allows scientists to calculate how much carbon dioxide will be released into the atmosphere. The carbon dioxide figures can then be plugged into GCMs to see what effect the added gas may have on future weather and climate.

Limitations of GCMs

Current models provide broad, generalized pictures of the future. Lots of specifics are missing. For example, they show that additional amounts of atmospheric carbon dioxide will lead to higher average global temperatures. But the models cannot predict how rising temperatures will affect atmospheric circulation patterns. Thus, they cannot tell which geographical areas will get warmer and which will get colder. They cannot be certain how much temperature change a specific area will experience. They cannot tell how precipitation patterns may be changed.

Many assumptions must be made in creating a model. For example, scientists know how much carbon dioxide has been produced by the burning of fossil fuels. But only about half of that carbon dioxide has shown up in the atmosphere. Where has the rest gone?

Much of the carbon dioxide has probably been absorbed by the oceans. What interactions occur between the oceans and the atmosphere? How do ocean currents, seasonal changes, salinity and other factors affect carbon dioxide levels and other aspects of the atmosphere? Much remains to be learned in this area. The forces at work in oceans aren't as well understood as those in the atmosphere. But to improve predictions of the future these forces should be part of a GCM.

The scientists who work with GCMs are the first to stress the weaknesses of their models. But GCMs are the best tools we have at the present time for predicting the future climate. And many climatologists believe that the models are providing quite a good picture of what might happen. James E. Hansen has pointed out that although models have become much more sophisticated in recent years, their conclusions about global warming haven't differed greatly from conclusions reached by models of the 1970s.

Conclusions

All of the conclusions agree that it's going to get warmer. At present, the average global temperature is 59° F (15° C). GCM simulations indicate that increasing concentrations of greenhouse gases are likely to cause this average temperature to jump by 3° to 8° F (1.7° to 4.4° C) by the middle of the next century. By that time, scientists expect that the concentrations of greenhouse gases will be at least twice what they were before the industrial revolution.

Let's look at two specific studies. A model at the National Center for Atmospheric Research in Colorado ran a simulation in which greenhouse gases increased by about 1% a year. The researcher found that under such conditions the lower atmosphere will warm by a global average of approximately 1°F (0.5°C) over the next 30 years. But, pointed out Warren M. Washington, "the warming is not equally distributed; some regions, mainly the continental interiors, become as much as 7°F (3.5°C) warmer."

The other simulations were conducted with a GCM at the British Meteorological Office. They demonstrate how changing a GCM can change its predictions. Initially, the GCM predicted that a doubling of carbon dioxide concentrations would cause an increase of 10.4°F (5.7°C) in average global temperature. But when the model was changed to simulate the amount of liquid water inside clouds, the predicted warming fell to 4.9°F (2.7°C). Does the latter present a truer picture of the effect clouds will have on climatic change? This is one of the unanswered questions that face atmospheric scientists as they try to make reliable predictions of the future.

Feedback Processes

Clouds are among the most important—and most complex—feedback mechanisms that must be considered in climate models. A feedback is a process in which the effect acts back upon the cause, thereby determining future behavior. Take a careless child who gets a burn as an example. The cause is putting a hand on a hot stove; the effect is a burn; the future behavior is taking care when near a stove. Another example is a thermostat. It senses the room temperature and feeds this information back to the heater. The heater is turned on or off so that the temperature is kept within the desired range.

Clouds may increase warming or they may slow it down. Because they are largely water vapor, they absorb radiation. This increases warming. But clouds also reflect solar radiation away from the Earth's surface. This minimizes warming. Do the two effects offset one another? Or is one effect dominant? Scientists are uncertain. Nor is it known how increased carbon dioxide and atmospheric changes affect clouds.

Perhaps as increased carbon dioxide levels cause the atmosphere to warm up, increased evaporation from the oceans will result in more clouds. The added clouds would block more sunlight and negate the warming effect of the increased carbon dioxide. But perhaps as the atmosphere warms, the oceans will also warm. Warm water can hold less carbon dioxide, so oceans will release carbon dioxide absorbed in the past. As this carbon dioxide enters the atmosphere, warming will accelerate.

Ice and snow also have feedback effects. They tend to reflect radiation, thereby reducing temperatures. But global warming will cause them to melt. Less radiation will be reflected. More will be absorbed by the soil and vegetation that take the place of the ice and snow.

Most global climate models incorporate some of the major feedback processes. But many others are not included. A study by Daniel A. Lashof of the U.S. Environmental Protection Agency concluded that if all feedback processes were considered, average global warming during the next century would range from 6.4° to 11.3° F (3.5° to 6.3° C). Because there are so many uncertainties, however, he noted that an increase of 14.4° F (8.0° C) or more might be possible.

Current Predictions

The astonishing number of interactions among the atmosphere, the oceans, plants, soil and other facets of our planet make it extremely difficult to predict exactly how much warming will occur. Scientists can offer only a range of predictions, rather than stating precisely how rapidly global warming will intensify.

Current predictions indicate that the amount of carbon dioxide in the atmosphere will be twice that of preindustrial levels by the year 2050. This is expected to cause temperatures to rise by 3° to 8° F (1.7° to 4.4° C), maybe more. But, if scientists are making significant errors in their models, those errors could just as easily be causing an underestimation of the amount of potential warming as an overestimation of it.

8
EFFECTS OF RISING TEMPERATURES

A rise in average global temperature of 3° to 8° F (1.7° to 4.4°C) may not seem like much. But it is expected to have profound effects. Definitive answers on what we can expect aren't possible, in part because nothing like this has ever been experienced in recorded history. In the past 10,000 years, the Earth has never had such a rapid rate of warming.

But while scientists may be uncertain on the degree of impact that warming will have, they agree that there definitely will be an impact—on weather patterns, ocean levels, agriculture, human health and other aspects of our world and our daily lives.

A Look to the Past

We can get some idea of the effects of climatic change by looking back to the Medieval Warm Period. This period extended from about 900 to 1200. Summer temperatures in northern Europe are believed to have averaged nearly 2° F (1.1° C) warmer than today. Alpine glaciers receded and vegetation grew hundreds of feet higher on mountains than today. Grapes were grown in places where late frosts now make vineyards impractical.

The northern seas were more easily navigable than today. Storms were rare and icebergs were seldom seen, even around

Opposite page: Global warming is expected to cause a dramatic rise in sea levels, which will be due—in large part—to increased temperatures that will melt glaciers.

Iceland. This was the time when Vikings settled Iceland, started a colony on the southwestern coast of Greenland and sailed westward to Labrador.

Not all areas enjoyed such mild weather. Despite the overall warming, winters were often bitterly cold. Record frosts hit the Mediterranean. The Tiber River in Rome and the Nile in Cairo froze over.

Precipitation patterns changed, too. Rainfall in the Mediterranean region increased. One piece of evidence of this is a bridge built in Palermo, Sicily, in 1113. It was built to span a river much wider than the one that flows there today.

In the American Midwest, it was a time of lushness. A group of Native Americans known as the Mill Creek people migrated to this prairie region about the year 900. They farmed the land, grew corn and other crops, and hunted deer and elk. Then, a drought hit the American Midwest—one that was to last for 200 years. The trees and tall grasses were replaced by short grasses that could survive on less water. The deer and elk, unable to find sufficient food, wandered off in search of greener pastures. The Mill Creek people turned to hunting buffalo, which grazed on the short grasses. But food was scarce because there wasn't enough water for farming. Slowly, the Mill Creek settlement wasted away.

Changing Climate and Weather Patterns

Much evidence exists that the climate changes in response to the greenhouse effect. The degree of change depends on the degree of global warming. Even the lowest projected temperature increases for the coming decades, however, are expected to cause considerable climatic changes. The greater the increase, the more drastic the changes.

Another factor affecting changes is the fact that a global temperature rise is not evenly distributed. Some parts of the Earth will warm more than other parts. Some parts may even become cooler. Global circulation models (GCMs) have shown that warming will be focused on polar and temperate zones. Temperatures will rise faster near the poles than near the equator.

WHY NOT ANOTHER ICE AGE?

Some people have predicted that our planet won't be getting warmer. They say that it will get colder. Another ice age is on the way, they believe, thanks to increasing carbon dioxide in the atmosphere, or in spite of it.

The scenarios vary. One suggests that increasing carbon dioxide will cause ocean temperatures to rise. This will result in more precipitation, more snow cover and the growth of glaciers. Another scenario suggests that as ocean temperatures increase, algae populations will boom. This will increase the reflection of heat, thus cooling the planet.

David Rind, an atmospheric scientist at NASA's Institute for Space Studies, has pointed out the fallacies of such suggestions. For example, glaciers are unlikely to grow in a warmer climate because glacial buildup occurs only when temperatures remain below freezing. "In most regions of the Northern Hemisphere this does not happen today; and it would be less possible in a warmer climate," states Rind. "If some feedback process initiated by the warming, such as a change in cloud cover or ocean reflectivity, acted to cool the climate, its importance would probably diminish as the warming diminished (for example, cloud cover would return to its current level), and so end the cooling."

Many scientists believe that ice ages only occur when there are changes in the Earth's spatial relationship to the sun. This theory was proposed in 1930 by the Yugoslavian geophysicist Milutin Milankovitch. He pointed out that three types of changes will affect the distance between the Earth and the sun: the shape of the Earth's orbit, the tilt of the polar axis and the alignment of the axis among the stars. Such changes happen over periods of many thousands of years. When they do occur, said Milankovitch, winters may become milder and summers may become cooler, favoring the formation of glaciers.

At the present time, changes in the Earth's orbit are causing less solar radiation to hit the Northern Hemisphere. But as Rind has pointed out, "it will be several thousand years before it reaches the minimum values which occurred during the last ice age.... The climate change that is our present concern is anticipated to be evident in the next decade, and to reach major proportions during the next one hundred years."

Such changes will have a significant effect on weather patterns. There will be changes in precipitation, storms, wind directions and so on. Some researchers believe our planet will be a wetter place. A GCM at NASA's Goddard Institute for Space Studies predicted that a doubling of carbon dioxide could increase humidity 30% to 40%.

Such increases will not occur uniformly around the world, however. Perhaps humid tropical areas will get even wetter while semi-arid regions will become drier. Several GCMs predict that rainfall in mid-latitudes such as the American Midwest will decrease, adversely affecting farming in those regions.

Rising temperatures are expected to increase tropical storm activity. The hurricane season in the Atlantic and Caribbean is expected to start earlier and last longer. Storms will be more severe. Changing wind patterns will mean that the paths of the storms will be changed, too, making some regions more vulnerable to damage than they are today.

NEW YORK, NEW YORK

Will global warming spell doom for our world? For life as we know it? Scientists aren't the only people pondering such questions. Novelists have also addressed these concerns. Their fictional scenarios warn us of what we may confront.

In the novel *Heat*, distinguished author Arthur Herzog considers the possible consequences of ascending carbon dioxide levels in the atmosphere. Near the book's end, engineer Lawrence Pick, too weak to move in the hot, humid weather, fantasizes about the future of New York City:

"Greatly shrunken by the rising sea, the city would resemble a huge Mayan ruin, with the tall buildings covered with creepers and moss. Perhaps crocodiles would float in the lakes and reservoirs, wild animals graze on streets carpeted with grass, vultures fly overhead. Around the city would be jungle inhabited by small bands of humans gradually reverting to savagery in suffocating heat that made civilized life impossible. Maybe hunting parties would come to the island in canoes over rivers swollen by the ocean, in search of food."

Many places will experience greater extremes between summer and winter temperatures. New York's summer temperatures are expected to rise, but in winter, brutal storms will sweep down from the north.

Tourist destinations may change as beaches flood and cities turn broiling or balmy. If average global temperatures rise several degrees, Washington, D.C., which now has 36 days each year above 90° F, (32° C) will have 87 days of such temperatures. Dallas, which now has 100 days above 90° F, will have 162. Will people still want to visit — or live in — these places?

Rising Seas

As the Earth gets warmer, there will be a rise in the average water level of the oceans. Two factors will cause this rise: thermal expansion and melting polar ice caps and glaciers.

As water is heated, it expands, or increases in volume. According to theory, global warming could cause thermal expansion of the ocean waters, which in turn would cause sea levels to rise.

Thermal expansion is expected to account for as much as half of the increase in sea level over the next century. The rest will come from the melting of glaciers. Glaciers are large, thick masses of slow-moving ice that persist from year to year. They cover about a tenth of the Earth's land surface. The vast ice sheets of Antarctica and Greenland account for most of this area. The ice sheet that covers most of Antarctica has an area of some 4,826,000 square miles (12,500,000 square kilometers). The one that extends over most of Greenland is about 695,000 square miles (1,800,000 square kilometers) in area. Smaller icecaps are found in Scandinavia, Baffin Island, Iceland and elsewhere. In addition, there are tens of thousands of valley glaciers that follow stream channels down mountain slopes. All together, glaciers contain about 75% of the available fresh water of the earth.

Because global warming is expected to be greatest in polar and temperate regions, scientists expect the glaciers to melt more rapidly than they do today.

An executive summary of a United Nations survey published in 1990 concluded that if worldwide "business as usual" continues, the resulting global temperature increase would produce a global mean sea-level rise of about 25 inches (0.6 meter) by the end of the next century. Other studies predict such increases will occur as soon as 2040. Much depends on how fast the polar ice melts. If global warming accelerates and the ice melts faster than expected, ocean levels may rise as much as 10 feet (3 meters) by 2100.

Antarctica

Coastal Areas

Rising sea levels will gradually flood low-lying coastal areas. In the United States, areas along the Atlantic Coast and Gulf of Mexico will be particularly affected. Much of the coast in this region is sinking. The combination of rising seas and sinking land (subsidence) will lead to flooding of extensive portions of the land. Louisiana, which is already losing 50 square miles (130 square kilometers) a year to rising seas and subsidence, will see much of its acreage disappear beneath the Gulf of Mexico. North Carolina has a very flat coastal plain; oceanographer Leonard J. Pietrafesa says "for every foot of increase in sea level, the shoreline will move [inland] 1,000 to 1,500 feet." At the western end of the nation, rising seas will drown Honolulu's international airport.

Beach erosion will be an increasing problem. The U.S. Environmental Protection Agency (EPA) has estimated that if the sea level rises 3 feet (0.9 meter), the nation will lose an area the size of Massachusetts—even if it spends more than $100 billion to protect critical shorelines. In addition to lost beaches, houses and other buildings that sit close to the water's edge will be undermined and destroyed.

Some scientists believe that more powerful storms, including hurricanes and monsoons, will be among the earliest symptoms of global warming. For example, the Atlantic hurricane season is expected to start earlier in the year, last longer and affect a larger area of the eastern United States. There may also be more frequent hurricanes. Coupled with rising sea levels, storms will cause severe property damage and loss of life. Waves will be higher, threatening to topple oil drilling platforms in the Gulf of Mexico. Storm surges (sudden onrushes of massive amounts of water) will wreak havoc, because the surges will build from a higher water level and increased erosion will remove natural storm barriers.

Seaside communities that now are flooded only once a century will be flooded more often. For instance, at the present time, 60% of Charleston, South Carolina, lies within an area likely to be flooded every 100 years; 20% lies within an area likely to be flooded every 10 years. A 3.3-foot (1-meter) rise in sea levels would put 45% of the city in the 10-year floodplain. A 5-foot (1.5-meter) rise would bring the figure to more than 60%. In such a case, what are now once-a-century floods would be likely to occur every 10 years.

The impact on some other countries will be even greater. In 1989, the U.N. Environment Programme identified 10 countries as "most vulnerable": Bangladesh, Egypt, Gambia, Indonesia, the Maldives, Mozambique, Pakistan, Senegal, Surinam and Thailand. Much of their land area is between 0 and 16 feet (5 meters) above mean sea level. In addition, these nations are densely populated and poor.

Heading the list is Bangladesh. More than half of the country lies at elevations of less than 16 feet (5 meters). Subsidence is a worsening problem. A study by John D. Milliman at Woods Hole Oceanographic Institution indicates that sea level rise in the delta area of Bangladesh may exceed 6.5 feet (2 meters) by 2050. This would cause heavy loss of agricultural lands, widespread displacement of people and catastrophic losses from storm surges.

Most of Egypt's 55 million people live crowded together on less than 4% of the land: the Nile River delta and the land that edges the river to the south. Subsidence, erosion and sea level rise are already causing marked loss of fertile land. According to Milliman's study, the Mediterranean Sea near Egypt will rise from 3.3 to 5 feet (1 to 1.5 meters) by 2050. This will make as much as 19% of Egypt's now-habitable land unlivable.

Wetlands

Areas other than lakes or rivers where the soil is saturated with water most of the year are called wetlands. Swamps, marshes and bogs are examples of wetlands. Some form inland; others are along the seacoast. They generally are home to a rich variety of plant and animal life. They hold excess water, which helps control flooding during heavy rains and which provides water reserves in times of drought.

Rising oceans would result in the loss of crucial coastal wetlands. According to the EPA, a 5-foot (1.5-meter) rise in sea level would mean a 30% net loss of coastal wetlands in the United States. Some parts of the country would be severely hit. For example, Louisiana currently has 2,874,600 acres (1,164,210 hectares) of wetlands. With a 5-foot sea-level rise, it would lose 2,306,900 acres (934,295 hectares), an 80% loss! The Pacific coastal states, which have only 89,100 acres (36,085 hectares) of coastal wetlands, would lose 36,300 acres (14,700 hectares). In other places, coastal flooding would create new wetlands. Florida, which now has 736,300 acres (298,200 hectares) of coastal wetlands, could gain 211,700 acres (85,740 hectares) if there were a 5-foot (1.5-meter) rise in sea level.

Shifting Habitats

If polar and temperate zones become warmer, there will be a poleward shift of ecological zones. Plant species that now live in a particular area will no longer be able to survive there. Whether a species will be trapped and die out depends on whether it will be able to migrate as fast as the temperature shifts. Many plant species—including many types of trees— cannot migrate very fast. They can move perhaps 1.2 miles (2 kilometers) a year. But if the ecological zones shift by 60 to 95 miles (100 to 150 kilometers) or more over the next 40 years, as some researchers predict, then there may be widespread extinction of plants.

As the ecological zones shift polewards, there may be a decrease in the amount of area suitable for forests, with a corresponding increase in grasslands and deserts. One group of researchers predicted a 17% increase in the amount of desert land in the world as a result of climate changes expected with a doubling of atmospheric carbon dioxide. This means a loss in productive land, both for agriculture and for habitats of a broad range of plants and animals. "If the climate models turn out to be right, the new world will be biologically less rich and less stable," said biologist Dennis Murphy of Stanford University.

In the United States, forests occupy about one-third of the land area. The warming trend will cause a decline in this figure. Much of the nation's southern forests will be lost and the range of species such as sugar maples and hemlocks is expected to shrink.

Many animals will be threatened, too. Animals that cannot move with the shifting ecological zones will perish, just as the woolly mammoth and other creatures became extinct during the last ice age. Snails and other slow-moving creatures will not be able to move fast enough. Shrimp, oysters and other animals that breed in estuaries—areas such as bays and river mouths, where fresh and salt water mix—will be killed by rising sea levels. Fish in tropical waters will die as temperatures rise. The caribou herds of the northern tundra will decline as their calving areas are inundated by rising seas. Species whose ranges have already been severely limited by farms and other human developments will also be at risk. This includes panthers and grizzly bears.

Moving Farms and Forests

The "amber waves of grain" of the American Midwest may be transformed into semiarid grasslands or even deserts as ecological zones in North America shift northward. Several climate models suggest that summer rainfall will decline in the area and droughts will become increasingly common. The nation's major grain crops—corn, wheat and soybeans—are strongly affected by precipitation and temperatures. Corn needs a lot of rain in July and, if possible, cooler-than-normal temperatures. Winter wheat needs the groundwater that is produced as snow melts. Soybeans, somewhat more resilient than corn or wheat, can recover from a July drought if there is adequate rainfall in August.

Rainfall is expected to decline in the Southwest, too, where farmers are largely dependent on irrigation water from dammed reservoirs. A study done by Dean F. Peterson Jr. of Utah State

The Solutions

A lush crop is the product of a healthy ecosystem.

Wind-powered generators spin in unison as the sun sets on Altamont Pass, California.

ENDING OUR DEPENDENCE on fossil fuels will slow the rate of global warming and buy precious time to devise ways to lessen the warming's effect. A variety of alternate energy sources exist. For example, huge turbine generators, clustered in "wind farms," can produce significant amounts of electricity.

Far right: Salicornia, which turns a brilliant red in the fall, can thrive in drought-plagued regions. Below: Insulating a home greatly improves its fuel efficiency.

CONSERVING ENERGY plays an important role in slowing global warming. Better home insulation, more fuel-efficient cars, energy-saving lights, recycling metals—these and other steps can make a significant difference. But many scientists agree that it is already too late to stop all warming. Thus, people are exploring ways of coping with higher temperatures, drought and diminished water supplies. For example, in drought regions, salicornia may be a substitute for soybeans and other fodder crops. One of salicornia's advantages: it can be irrigated with seawater.

SAVING OUR FORESTS would significantly reduce the effects of carbon dioxide emissions. Recycling paper can save millions of trees every year. In addition, large areas sorely need to be reforested. New forests would store carbon, serve as needed habitats for wildlife and ensure a healthier, richer world for future generations.

Left: Giant rolls of recycled paper are wheeled through a factory in Minnesota. *Overleaf:* Tiny pine seedlings are planted carefully by hand in Washington, near the Puget Sound.

BLACK BLIZZARDS

The first one struck in November 1933. From Montana across the plains to Illinois, vast quantities of dust were swept high into the sky. Winds carried the huge duststorm eastward. "Black rain" fell in New York. "Brown snow" covered the hills of Vermont.

Such "black blizzards" continued to ravage the American Midwest throughout the 1930s as the region suffered sweltering heat waves and earth-cracking droughts. July temperatures in the corn belt states averaged 2° to 4°F (1.1° to 2.2°C) or more above normal. July precipitation—essential for corn growth—averaged only 50% to 85% of normal. The effects of the heat and drought were made even worse by overgrazing and poor agricultural practices, which exposed the topsoil and led to its erosion by the relentless winds.

Some 50 million acres (20 million hectares) of once-rich land were turned into a huge dust bowl. Few crops were able to survive. Those that did were withered and stunted. Cattle died of starvation or suffocated in the swirling dust. Some 15,000 people were killed by respiratory illnesses and the sweltering temperatures. Thousands more abandoned their homes and fled to other parts of the country.

While the Midwest dried up, other parts of the country were experiencing record rains and floods. In March 1936, New England was drenched. Most of downtown Hartford, Connecticut, was flooded as the Connecticut River crested at 37.6 feet (11.4 meters)—8.6 feet (2.6 meters) higher than any time in the previous 300 years. In January 1937, it was the Ohio River Valley's turn. At Cincinnati, Ohio, the water rose almost 9 feet (2.7 meters) higher than any previously known crest.

Many scientists fear the extreme weather conditions that plagued the United States during the 1930s may be an example of what is to come as heat-trapping gases build up in the atmosphere and cause changes in climate and global weather patterns.

University and Andrew A. Keeler of Keller-Bliesner Engineering looked at the effects on crop production of a warming of 3°F (1.7°C) combined with a 10% drop in precipitation. They found that the viable land in arid regions of the western states would decrease by nearly one-third.

Farming in the Southeast would also be devastated. The EPA has warned that soybean and corn yields in the Southeast could fall by 90% or more. And without irrigation, as much as 50% of the land there would not be fit for cultivation.

Croplands will increase in the northern Great Plains, the northern Great Lakes states and the Pacific Northwest. Production of grain crops is expected to shift to these areas. And crops now grown in the northern United States may shift into Canada. Apples, an important crop in Washington, require winter cooling to flower and bear fruit. If the area becomes too warm, the trees will not be productive.

Another country with a productive "breadbasket" is the Soviet Union. Its vast grain-growing regions are also likely to experience higher temperatures and less precipitation.

On the positive side, some scientists believe that increased amounts of carbon dioxide in the air may boost the yield of some crops, since plants need carbon dioxide for photosynthesis. The gas has been used for years by growers of greenhouse tomatoes. And laboratory experiments showed that doubling carbon dioxide levels increases corn yields by 16%, wheat and rice yields by 36% and cotton yields by a whopping 80%. However, any comparable gains in the field may be overwhelmed by damage from excessive heat and increased amounts of ultraviolet radiation. For instance, rice—the staple for more than half the world's people—is especially vulnerable to ultraviolet radiation. There are also the problems of increasingly erratic weather; increased pollution; poor soils; declining water for irrigation; and booming populations of wheat rust and other pests and diseases that thrive in hot, dry weather.

A 1988 EPA report said: "On a national scale, the supply of agricultural commodities does not appear to be threatened by climate change." A similar assessment was reported in 1990 by economist Richard M. Adams of Oregon State University and nine colleagues. They fed data from two climate models into a model of U.S. agriculture, to simulate how grain crops would respond to climate changes. Results: no apparent reason to anticipate major catastrophic effects or food shortages during the next 50 years.

Not everyone agrees. There may well be sufficient food to feed Americans. But currently the nation exports large amounts of grain—grain that many other nations depend upon for their people's survival. Drought, the need to shift to new farmlands and other problems may reduce such exports.

And if droughts occur too often or last for too many years, perhaps the United States will not even be able to feed itself. In 1988, a summer drought coupled with a July heat wave cut U.S. corn production by 45%. Overall, grain production suffered its largest decrease since the 1930s. For the first time in history, Americans consumed more grain than they produced. They paid more, too. The drought contributed to price hikes for cereals, breads and other foods. Computer simulations indicate that a 3°F (1.7°C) rise in global temperatures would quadruple the occurrence of crop-damaging heat waves.

Declining Water Supplies

The warming trend will probably cause changes in water quantity and quality in some areas. This will affect drinking supplies as well as the water needs of industry and agriculture.

One area at risk is the Ogallala Aquifer. This huge underground lake provides irrigation water for millions of acres of land between South Dakota and Texas. Overpumping has severely depleted the aquifer's water reserves. Experts warn that many parts of the aquifer will be drained by early in the 21st century—just when droughts caused by global warming will increase the need to tap such reservoirs.

Another area at risk is California, which is already experiencing water difficulties. Global warming could cause an earlier melting of snow in the mountains that supply much of the state's water. This could mean that less water will be available in the late summer, typically a dry period in much of the state.

In many places, the purity of drinking water could decline. For instance, rising sea levels may contaminate water supplies as seawater migrates up rivers. A 2-foot (0.6-meter) rise in sea level would inundate Philadelphia's water intakes along the Delaware River, making the water too salty to drink.

Demand for irrigation water will rise. But a combination of diminishing water supplies, growing populations, aging irrigation systems and rising costs of new water projects may cause per-capita irrigated agriculture to decline. A study by Sandra Postel, vice president for research at the Worldwatch Institute, showed that during most of the 20th century per-capita irrigated agriculture expanded faster than world population. By 1978, it had reached 1.18 acres (0.48 hectares). But since 1978, there has been a decline of approximately 6% in per-capita irrigated lands. Today, these areas are growing at about half the rate of the population. They account for only 17% of the total area under cultivation. Yet irrigated lands provide 33% of the global harvest. If these percentages don't increase, food supplies may soon be jeopardized.

Competition over diminishing water supplies will become fierce. It will pit people against people, state against state,

WATER FIGHT

An example of the type of battle that will become commonplace as water scarcity increases occurred in 1990 along the Missouri River. Almost three years of drought brought demands from Iowa, Kansas and other downstream areas that more water be released from upstream reservoirs in northern states. The water was needed, people said, to irrigate farms, generate electricity, supply community water systems and keep barge traffic moving. But South Dakota, supported by North Dakota and Montana, won a suit to limit releases during the critical spawning period of the walleye, a popular game fish and a basis of the area's economically important sports fishing and recreational industry. This tale has a happy ending, at least for the moment: Heavy downstream rains gave both sides a reprieve.

Dramatic climate changes and rising seas can potentially destroy much of the Earth's now fertile land and cause widespread famine and drought.

nation against nation. Industries will shift to areas with sufficient water. Communities in areas with insufficient water, such as Phoenix and Los Angeles, will stop growing. And agriculture is likely to suffer. "Where scarcities loom," said Postel, "cities and farms are beginning to compete for available water; when supplies tighten, farmers typically lose out."

Weaker, Sicker People

Heat waves extract a physical toll on people. The heat puts a strain on the heart, as the body tries to cool itself. The heart works harder than usual, pumping more blood to the tiny blood vessels in the skin. There, heat carried by the blood is given off to the surrounding air, thus cooling the body. When the air temperature is as high or higher than the body temperature, however, getting rid of heat is a problem. Bodily processes slow down in an effort to limit heat production. But this makes the person more susceptible to infections.

Global warming is also expected to further increase ground-level ozone pollution and smog formation. Coupled with the heat, this will cause an increasing number of deaths from respiratory problems such as asthma and emphysema. The people most at risk will be those in poor health to begin with, such as the elderly and the poor.

At the same time that people's immune systems are harmed, there may be a faster spread of diseases. Most infectious diseases are not expected to be influenced by global warming. But diseases carried by insects, such as malaria, are likely to spread as warmer weather expands the insects' range.

Social, Economic and Political Effects

Climate changes, sea level rises and other direct effects of greenhouse warming can be expected to have major social, economic and political effects. Consider the farmers of the American Midwest. As agricultural productivity declines in states such as Iowa, people's incomes will fall and jobs will decline. Should these people be compensated? How? Should people in states that benefit from global warming be charged for this "luck"?

Answering such questions becomes even thornier when viewed on an international scale. Who is to help people in nations such as Bangladesh as their lands are lost beneath rising seas? How do we deal with mass migrations of people from lands that have turned to desert? What support do we give to governments whose stability is threatened by scarcity of food and water?

GLOBAL WARMING AROUND THE WORLD
European Countries (14%)
China (7%)
USSR (14%)
Brazil (4%)
India (4%)
United States (21%)
Rest of the World (36%)

Has Global Warming Already Begun?

With world temperatures already significantly warmer than a century ago, some scientists contend that global warming due to the greenhouse effect has already begun. Testifying before a congressional committee in 1988—the hottest year on record—James E. Hansen, director of NASA's Institute for Space Studies, said: "Global warming has reached a level such that we can ascribe with a high degree of confidence a cause and effect relationship between the greenhouse effect and observed warming . . . It is already happening now."

Climatic Events

Periods of climatic stress are generally marked by extreme weather conditions: memorable cold waves and blistering heat, lengthy droughts and destructive floods. We've experienced a lot of such weather in recent years.

The 1980s was the hottest decade on record, with 6 of the 10 warmest years between 1890 and 1989. There were costly droughts in the American Midwest. In California, more than three consecutive years of drought forced water rationing in some areas. In 1988, violent wind storms in Great Britain knocked down thousands of massive trees. In 1989, Hurricane Hugo battered Puerto Rico and other Caribbean islands and parts of the eastern United States.

The problems continued into 1990. In February, gale-force winds struck Western Europe, disrupting transportation, tearing down roofs and power lines, and killing more than 50 people. In May, ferocious floods—exactly the kind that computer models predict will occur during global warming—struck Arkansas, Texas, Oklahoma and four other states. In June, the Southwest blistered under record temperatures, including a high of 122° F (50° C) in Phoenix.

Glaciers and Arctic Snow

For the first time since its discovery in 1841, large parts of Antarctica's Ross Ice Shelf have been breaking away. One of these massive icebergs is as large as the state of Delaware! At the other end of the Earth, snow has been melting earlier and earlier in the Arctic. In the 1940s, snow often remained on the ground until mid-June. Today, the land is free of snow by late May or even earlier.

Sea Changes

Records from tide gauges situated around the world show that sea levels have risen by 4 to 8 inches (10 to 20 centimeters) over the past century. By itself, this does not indicate that the oceans are rising. Tide gauges only indicate the relative levels between coastline and water. If a coastline moves up or down while the ocean stays the same, a gauge will still indicate a change in sea level. Various geological effects can influence relative sea levels. One such effect is called glacial rebound. As ice age glaciers melt, the land they covered, no longer weighed down by the heavy ice, rises to its former level.

W. Richard Peltier and A. Mark Tushingham of the University of Toronto used a computer model to calculate glacial rebound around the world. When they subtracted these figures from the tide gauge readings, they found that sea levels have been rising at an average rate of 0.1 inch (2.4 millimeters) a year. Although land mass uplift, subsidence and other effects may also be altering sea levels, the two scientists believe the fairly uniform annual increase "is strongly suggestive of the action of ongoing glacier and ice sheet melting." Though their work does not prove that global warming due to the greenhouse effect is occurring, it would not be surprising, they point out, if "the greenhouse effect were first observed through an indirect response such as an increase in global sea level."

Health

In Kenya, malarial mosquitoes are native to the hot lowlands. But they have migrated to the cool highlands. "There are strong indications that their presence is one of the results of the greenhouse effect," said environmentalist Herik Othieno of Kenya.

9

Adapting to Changes

Even if people around the world were to take immediate steps to counteract warming, some warming would occur. "We are already irrevocably committed to major global change in the years ahead," reported the National Academy of Sciences in 1989. "The elevated concentrations of greenhouse gases produced to date by human activities will persist for many centuries and will slowly change the climate of the earth, regardless of our actions."

The evolutionary aspects of global warming are important to remember. It's not a process that will happen suddenly, causing radical changes overnight. It's occurring now, slowly, almost imperceptibly.

The National Academy of Sciences is among the groups that recommend that people begin to explore and institute ways of coping with global warming. By taking action now, it may be possible to lessen some of the damage caused by higher temperatures, rising seas and prolonged droughts. An early start is essential because many actions involve significant amounts of time. Dikes to protect against rising seas cannot be built overnight. Nor can researchers quickly develop new strains of drought-resistant crops. If we wait until disaster is near, it may be too late to avoid catastrophic damage.

However, because of the uncertainty of how much warming will occur, when it will occur and what effects it will have,

Opposite page: The long-term survival of life on this planet depends on our ability to adapt to the constant ebb and flow of natural forces.

flexibility is critical, said the National Academy of Sciences. For instance, we do not know how precipitation patterns may change. Therefore, it is best to try to prepare for a variety of possibilities. "Policies need to be successful under a wide variety of contingencies, including a scenario in which no change in climate occurs," commented Joel B. Smith of the U.S. Environmental Protection Agency.

Adaptations are not the only answer, of course. At the same time, we must take steps to slow production of greenhouse gases.

Protecting Coastal Areas

Rapidly increasing sea levels pose threats to beaches, wetlands, buildings and freshwater supplies. A variety of adaptations can limit damage caused by the rising water.

Limiting Coastal Development

Restricting building in coastal areas will have at least three important benefits. First, it will limit the cost of protecting such properties as sea levels rise. Second, it will limit the potential disasters to lives and property arising from more frequent, more powerful hurricanes. Third, it will allow wetlands and beaches to migrate inland, reestablishing themselves and thus continuing to provide habitats for fish and other wildlife.

One measure is to require that new construction be set back from the shoreline a distance equal to the width of land expected to be lost to erosion in a given number of years. Maine has a set-back requirement of 100 years. Maine also requires property owners to assume responsibility for moving structures as the oceans rise.

Protecting Shorelines

Dikes, levees and other protective walls can be built in places where land and buildings need to be protected. Sand can be hauled onto beaches to combat erosion—a practice already common in many communities.

DUTCH FORESIGHT

As people around the world prepare to defend their coastlines against rising seas, they are turning to the Dutch for guidance. Since the Middle Ages, the Dutch have been reclaiming land from the sea. Much of their country exists because of dikes, windmills and pumps.

A dike is a long barrier built to prevent flooding. A sea dike is usually 10 to 16 feet (3 to 5 meters) above the storm flood level. The side facing the ocean is made of erosion-resistant materials such as concrete blocks cemented together with asphalt. Protruding stones or built-in steps on the outer face reduce the length of waves as they run up against the wall. Watertight concrete chambers called caissons are often used to form the base of the dike, and the entire structure may be reinforced with steel.

Originally in the Netherlands, windmills were used to keep the water level of reclaimed land under control. Today, steam, diesel and electric pumps are more common, removing excess water in winter and pumping in water during the summer dry season.

Planning for rising sea levels is already well advanced in the Netherlands. The nation's dikes and other coastal defenses—developed over hundreds of years—are capable of coping with an additional 3.3-foot (1-meter) rise in sea level without major difficulties. Nonetheless, they will be strengthened and expanded. Rivers and canals will be changed to prevent seawater from penetrating the soil and ruining water supplies and farmland. The cost will be high. Studies indicate that an investment of as much as $10 billion will be needed to protect the Netherlands from a 3.3-foot (1-meter) sea-level rise.

Like the United States, the Netherlands is a wealthy nation. It can afford to defend itself against the rising seas. Other countries are not as fortunate. "We can cope," said ecologist Gjerrit P. Hekstra. "But not Indonesia, not Bangladesh, not Vietnam. They don't have the resources to do it. Who's going to pay the bill for the developing countries?"

Other Measures

To prevent contamination of drinking water supplies by seawater migrating up rivers, it will be necessary to move water intakes or build barrier dams to divert the salt water. Steps will have to be taken to prevent leaching from landfills, particularly hazardous-waste disposal sites, that are likely to flood. Canals, rivers, ship channels and other waterways will have to be restructured. Out at sea, oil drilling platforms will have to be raised.

Maintaining Farms and Forests

As the Earth warms, farmers may be able to adapt by switching to crops that are better suited to higher temperatures and lower soil moisture. Some of these crops already exist. For instance, a succulent called salicornia may be a substitute for soybeans and other fodder crops in drought regions. One of its advantages is that it can be irrigated with seawater.

Other crops are being developed in the laboratory using genetic engineering techniques. Some of these techniques are centuries old. For instance, corn has been selectively bred for some 7,000 years. Other techniques, such as recombinant-DNA procedures, are recent developments. Recombinant-DNA, also known as gene splicing, involves the transfer of bits of genetic material from one organism to another. By inserting desirable genes from one species into another, it is possible to develop improved plant breeds at a much faster pace than the traditional cross-breeding methods.

Plant scientists are stepping up efforts to develop heat-resistant and drought-resistant crops and trees. In Israel, researchers have successfully grown fruits and nuts at temperatures as high as 115° F (46° C). In the United States, scientists have used genetic engineering to produce poplars designed to be grown on plantations for energy production. The trees, which grow rapidly, could be burned to provide energy or converted into ethanol to run automobiles.

Genetic engineering offers phenomenal potential. For example, in the not-distant future, it may be possible to transfer bacterial genes responsible for nitrogen-fixing into corn and other crop plants. Then the world could become much less dependent on fertilizers.

Scientists stress that it is essential to maintain genetic diversity. The future is uncertain. It is not clear which strain of wheat, which variety of maple, which breed of catfish will be best suited for each new environment that is created. By depending on only a single variety of an organism, our flexibility to deal with change is greatly limited.

Safeguarding Water Supplies

Global warming will cause droughts in many areas. During these dry spells, people will depend on water stored in reservoirs and beneath the ground—water that fell in previous years. Already, many of these water supplies are being used faster than they are replenished. Efforts need to be made to conserve the water and to institute methods that use water more wisely. The faster this is done, the bigger the water "safety net" we will have if drought conditions become commonplace.

Conservation

Studies have shown that residential water use could easily be cut by a third through currently available methods. For example, attaching a low-flow faucet aerator to a faucet reduces water flow by 50%. But because the device mixes air into the water as it leaves the tap, the flow actually seems stronger. If every American home installed faucet aerators, the nation would save an estimated 250 million gallons (950 million liters) or more of water every day!

Another wasteful user of water in homes is the toilet. The standard American toilet uses 5 to 7 gallons (19 to 26 liters) every time it is flushed. In contrast, ultra low-flush toilets empty the bowl using only 0.5 to 1.5 gallons (2 to 5 liters) of water. Until it is time to invest in a new toilet, however, people can reduce the amount of water used by their current system with displacement devices and dams. These reduce the amount of water held by the tank, cutting annual water use by thousands of gallons.

Modern technologies and better management practices allow farmers to make more efficient use of water supplies. Low-energy precision application (LEPA), for example, delivers water closer to the ground and in larger drops than traditional sprinkler systems. This decreases the amount of water lost to evaporation. Farmers in Texas cut the average amount of irrigation water they used by 28% between 1974 and 1987 because they adopted LEPA and other practices.

Another step is reducing government water subsidies so that users are encouraged to invest in more efficient practices. In the United States, the federal government supplies water to more than 10 million acres (4 million hectares) of irrigated land in the western states. Such subsidies, pointed out Sandra

Postel, vice president for research at the Worldwatch Institute, discourage conservation. She commented in 1990:

"Since agriculture uses such an enormous quantity of water, conserving even a small portion of it can meet a large share of new urban needs. Raising water prices to reflect the true cost of deliveries is a critical step toward this end. The Federal Bureau of Reclamation supplies water to a quarter of the West's irrigated land under long-term contracts at greatly subsidized prices. Farmers benefiting from one huge California project, for example, have repaid only about 5% of the costs over the last 40 years. Hundreds of federal contracts are coming up for renewal. If the bureau seizes this opportunity to set prices that prompt farmers to conserve water, stresses in the West could ease measurably."

The problem is not limited to the United States. Government subsidies in most developing nations cover 80% to 90% of the cost of delivering water. In Pakistan, for example, fees paid by farmers cover about 13% of the government's costs.

Reclaimed Water

Americans produce billions of gallons of sewage every day. It is treated in chemical sewage treatment plants, then disposed of, mainly by pouring it into the nearest river or ocean. But according to researchers at Pennsylvania State University, untreated sewage averages out to be 99.9% pure water. Instead of discarding this resource, it could be treated, then used to irrigate crops. This practice has proven highly successful in Europe, Australia and Israel. By the end of the 1990s, Israel plans to reuse 80% of its wastewater. Currently, the nation reuses 35% of its municipal wastewater, mostly for irrigation. Approximately 37,000 acres (15,000 hectares), most of them cotton fields, are irrigated with this reclaimed water.

Desalination

Making fresh water out of seawater could help meet the water needs of people living on islands and in coastal cities. Today, highly automated systems are available that extract fresh water from seawater at significantly lower costs than traditional systems.

Middle Eastern nations, particularly Kuwait, Saudi Arabia, the United Arab Emirates, Qatar and Bahrain, account for some 65% of the desalination market—a market that is expected to grow steadily in coming years as plants are needed in arid regions where population is rising.

Meeting Energy Needs

As the number of hot summer days increase in places like New York and Los Angeles, residents of those communities will want to increase their use of air conditioning. The Electric Power Research Institute calculated that for every increase of 1.8°F (.99°C) in temperature, summer power demand in New York City will raise 2% to 3%. This will have a sizable impact on the region's already limited generating capacity. The electric power industry must determine how to handle such demands. Conservation, new technologies and pricing policies appear to be part of the solution.

Migrating Organisms

As climate zones shift toward the poles, many plants and animals will have to migrate in order to survive. This will be difficult for many organisms, for two reasons. First, climate changes may be rapid, creating a particular problem for slow movers such as snails. Second, migration routes may be blocked by farms, roads, towns and other human construction. Grizzly bears and elk are among the animals already hemmed in by human development. The added stresses of warming climate could doom them.

Joel B. Smith of the U.S. Environmental Protection Agency points out: "One way to facilitate migration and reduce the loss of plants and animals is to use migration corridors. Greenways and hedgerows are examples of corridors that would allow plants and animals to migrate as climate changes. Corridors should also be opened between wildlife refuges to reduce fragmentation of parks and reserves. Migratory corridors have short-term benefits in that they provide recreational opportunities for people and expanded habitats for wildlife."

10

THE NEED TO CONSERVE ENERGY

How rapidly global warming occurs depends to some degree on people's efforts. The more carbon dioxide and other greenhouse gases we pump into the atmosphere, the faster the warming. Therefore, our immediate goal should be to slow the rate of warming. This will buy precious time—to do more research, anticipate problems before they occur, devise ways to mitigate the warming's effects.

Save the Fossils

Fossil fuels—coal, oil and natural gas—are our main energy sources. They supply about 88% of the world's energy. Burning these fuels is the major source of atmospheric carbon dioxide. If we are to limit greenhouse gas emissions, we must limit the use of fossil fuels.

Industrialized nations are the major consumers, using more than 70% of the world's energy. Among these nations, the United States is number one. The nation uses twice as much energy per unit of gross national product as West Germany or Sweden, and more than twice as much as Switzerland or Denmark.

Much of this energy is used to operate our automobiles. Up to 40% of the oil used in the United States each year is consumed by automobiles. The amount of carbon dioxide produced is enormous: Every gallon of gasoline burned adds 19 pounds of carbon dioxide to the atmosphere.

Opposite page: Solar energy is a safe, nonpolluting alternative to fossil fuels. It is unlimited in supply and is readily available to anyone who has the equipment to use it.

Global warming and other environmental problems aren't the only impetus for ending our dependence on fossil fuels. There's the additional problem of limited supplies. The world is running out of fossil fuels. By the end of the 21st century, most of the world's oil and natural gas reserves may have been used up. Coal reserves are expected to last longer, but they too may be gone in several hundred years.

"Ours is the generation that may have to act, and act courageously, to phase out our accustomed reliance on fossil fuels . . . If we harbor any sense of responsibility toward preserving spaceship Earth, and toward the welfare of our progeny, we can scarcely afford to leave the carbon dioxide problem to the next generation," commented J. Murray Mitchell Jr. of the U.S. Environmental Data Information Service (a division of the National Oceanic and Atmospheric Administration).

Mitchell made his appeal in 1977. In the intervening years, there have been some positive developments. Conservation measures taken by industrialized nations since the early 1970s have markedly cut the amount of energy used to produce a unit of gross national product. The U.S. gross national product grew 40% between 1973 and 1985. But because of conservation, the nation's total energy consumption remained constant during those years.

Many experts believe that industrialized nations may continue to curb their exponential growth rate of fossil fuel use. But developing nations are expected to significantly increase their use of these fuels over the coming decades as they seek to industrialize, improve living standards and accommodate their fast-growing populations. For example, China has extensive coal reserves that it plans to exploit in its efforts to modernize its economy.

Conservation is for everyone. Individuals, communities, industries, governments—all have important roles to play in conserving energy. Individuals can walk or bicycle rather than jumping into cars for a short drive to shops or work. Communities can provide mass transit systems and insist on recycling of paper, metals and other materials. Industries can

A JOB FOR UNCLE SAM

Government initiative is essential to develop, institute and enforce changes designed to cut greenhouse gas emissions. For instance, cars, trucks and other road vehicles account for nearly 75% of the energy used for transportation. One way to control these vehicles' contribution to the greenhouse effect is to improve efficiency. Deborah Bleviss, executive director of the International Institute for Energy Conservation says:

"[The government's] practice of setting progressively tighter fuel-economy standards has worked in the past and could work again. By the end of the century, an average new-car fuel economy of 45 miles per gallon and an average light-truck fuel economy of 35 miles per gallon are feasible goals, and aggressive enough to have a substantial impact on reducing CO_2 emissions.

"The government also needs to offer incentives to consumers to buy fuel-efficient cars. Strengthening the existing tax on the purchase of gas 'guzzlers' and offering a financial incentive for the purchase of gas 'sippers' are two strategic initiatives."

---

remodel buildings, change raw materials, and revise processes to be more energy efficient. Governments can use tax incentives to encourage conservation, and tax increases to discourage wasteful practices.

Fuel savings can be enormous. One of the best examples is the recycling of aluminum. By substituting recycled scrap for virgin materials in the manufacture of aluminum, a 95% energy savings is realized! Making a ton of aluminum from virgin material uses 51,369 kilowatts of energy. Using recycled material requires only 2,000 kilowatts.

Today, scrap aluminum is an important supply source for aluminum producers and fabricators. Some of the scrap aluminum comes from industrial sources. Some comes from obsolete products, including airplanes, machinery and automobiles. Some comes from recycled household goods such as soda cans, frozen food trays and pie plates.

In 1989, Americans recycled 60.8% of their all-aluminum beverage cans—a record 49.4 billion cans. Recycling these cans and other scrap aluminum saved more than 12 billion kilowatt hours of electricity, according to the Aluminum Association. That is the energy equivalent of some 20 million barrels of oil!

Even the recycling of a single can has a significant impact on energy conservation. "Throwing away an aluminum beverage container wastes as much energy as filling the same can half full of gasoline and pouring it out on the ground," points out William U. Chandler of the Worldwatch Institute.

Improving Efficiency

Another way to conserve fossil fuels is to improve efficiency. For example, a more efficient automobile uses less fuel to travel greater distances. A more efficient light bulb produces more light while using less electricity.

"There are many inefficiencies in the way we use energy," commented William K. Reilly, head of the U.S. Environmental Protection Agency. "Together, these inefficiencies add up to a substantial and costly, yet correctable, share of the emissions that contribute to climate change and other environmental problems."

Fuel-Efficient Autos

By increasing the average fuel efficiency of cars, gasoline consumption can be cut dramatically. In 1974, new autos averaged 14.4 miles per gallon. In 1989, the figure was 28.3 miles per gallon—a slight decline from the 1988 high of 28.7 miles per gallon. Much greater efficiency is technologically possible. For instance, reducing the weight of a typical auto could save 25% of the energy it uses. Advanced engines, such as ceramic gas turbines, would also increase efficiency.

Data from the Environmental Action Foundation indicates that a car getting 18 miles per gallon of gasoline emits 58 tons of carbon dioxide over its lifetime. A car averaging 27.5 miles per gallon emits 38 tons. A car averaging 45 miles per gallon emits 23 tons. And a car averaging 60 miles per gallon emits only 17 tons. This higher efficiency is possible now. Volvo, for example, has produced a prototype that gets 81 miles per gallon on the highway and 63 in the city. The car seats four people and meets U.S. crash-safety requirements.

Energy-Efficient Buildings

Impressive energy savings can be realized from remodeling buildings to reduce energy use. This is true for every type of building. Installing storm or thermal windows and doors, adding extra insulation, using new solar-heating systems, adding caulking or weatherstripping around windows and doors—these are but a few of the steps that save on energy bills and limit carbon dioxide emissions.

Communities can encourage energy conservation by adopting building standards that require developers to construct more efficient buildings. Tax breaks can also help, say for installing heat pumps. A heat pump is a device that uses outside air for both heating and cooling a building. It is highly efficient because over 50% of the heating energy it supplies comes from outside, rather than from a fossil fuel.

Improved Appliances

Among the steps that improve the efficiency of appliances are better heat-transfer techniques, more efficient motors, better insulation and greater surface areas on refrigerant coils.

The U.S. Federal Trade Commission requires that appliances carry labels tagged "EnergyGuide." The label spells out an appliance's estimated yearly energy costs. It also lists the lowest and highest energy costs for models of similar size also on the market. More energy-efficient models may be more expensive initially but they cost less to operate. For example, one washing machine model may have a purchase price of $500 and an estimated yearly operating cost of $34. A second model, of equal size, may have a purchase price of $250 and an estimated annual operating cost of $163. Although the second machine costs $250 less to purchase, it will cost $1,419 more to operate over the product's expected 11-year lifetime. Or to look at it another way, in less than two years the first model's energy savings will justify its higher purchase price.

Energy-Saving Lights

Lighting consumes huge amounts of energy, particularly when considered together with the air conditioning needed to offset heat generated by inefficient lights. Yet many highly efficient lighting products are available. "When fully used, these products will save consumers over $25 billion per year and prevent the annual generation of hundreds of millions of tons of carbon dioxide in addition to substantial reductions of sulfur dioxide and nitrous oxide pollutants," notes Congresswoman Claudine Schneider of Rhode Island.

GREEN INSULATION

Studies have shown that landscaping can conserve energy. The proper placement of trees and shrubs can lower a home's heating and cooling use by 25% or more. In addition, trees absorb carbon dioxide as they grow.

But the amount of carbon dioxide absorbed by a tree is surpassed by the amount it prevents from entering the atmosphere as a result of burning fuels. According to research done by scientists at Lawrence Berkeley Laboratory, a tree that provides shade and cooling indirectly causes reductions in carbon dioxide emissions equivalent to 15 times the amount of carbon dioxide the tree alone can absorb!

Evergreen trees, such as pines and cedars, provide shade all year around. Deciduous trees, such as maples and oaks, shed their leaves in the autumn; they provide shade during the hot summer months but let the sun in during the winter months. In addition, trees provide protection from the wind.

Dense shrubs such as hemlock can provide good energy savings when planted on east, west and north exposures. The shrubs, if 4 feet (1.2 meters) or taller, create shade, block winds and provide insulating dead air spaces between the plants and the home.

One such product is the compact fluorescent lamp. An 18-watt compact provides as much light as a conventional 75-watt bulb. But it uses less than one-fourth as much energy. It costs more—about $20—but it lasts about 10,000 hours. In comparison, a conventional bulb costs about $1 but lasts only 750 hours. Over its lifetime, the compact saves the consumer most or even all of its cost. Plus, because it uses less electricity, it prevents the generation of a ton of carbon dioxide and 25 pounds (11 kilograms) of sulfur dioxide.

Switching to highly efficient lights and other energy-saving devices can thus eliminate or at least slow our growing population's need for more and more costly, polluting, resource-depleting electric power plants. "A mid-sized facility producing 2 million compacts per year costs $7 million to set up and over its lifetime will displace the need for a 350-megawatt coal plant with a capital cost in excess of $300 million," points out Schneider.

Energy-Saving Tips for the Home

Most residential energy, 70%, is used to heat and cool homes. Another 20% is used to heat water. The remaining 10% is used for lighting, cooking and running small appliances. What does this mean in terms of carbon dioxide emissions? Here are some examples of how much carbon dioxide you add

Appliance	*Pounds of CO_2 added to atmosphere*
Television set, color	.64 lb./hour
Steam iron	.85 lb./hour
Vacuum cleaner	1.70 lb./hour
Air conditioner, room	4.00 lb./hour
Ceiling fan	4.00 lb./day
Refrigerator, frost-free	12.80 lb./day
Waterbed heater	24.00 lb./day
with thermostat	12.80 lb./day
Dishwasher	2.60 lb./load
Clothes dryer	10.00 lb./load

to the atmosphere when you use electrical appliances. (The data assumes the electricity was generated by burning coal.)

There are many ways to cut energy use in the home. For instance, if every American raised air-conditioning temperatures by 6° F (3.3° C), the United States would save the equivalent of 190,000 barrels of oil a day!

Here are some energy-conserving tips:
- Make sure your home is tight and well-insulated.
- Draft-proof windows and doors. Use weatherstripping. Maintain caulking. Switch to double glazed windows (two panes of glass separated by a sealed air space). Install storm windows and doors. Use tight-fitting drapes or blinds.
- Periodically clean and service your heating system.
- Maintain the water heater. Drain a bucket of water out of the bottom of the heater tank once or twice a year, to remove sediment. Place a layer of insulation around the tank.
- Insulate exposed pipes to prevent heat loss from hot pipes and sweating from cold pipes.
- Take showers rather than tub baths. An average person uses about half as much hot water in a shower as in a bath.
- Turn heating thermostats down in winter and air conditioner thermostats up in summer.
- Keep the air conditioner filter clean. When the air conditioner is not being used for long periods of time, place a cover over the outside to stop drafts.
- Choose efficient lighting fixtures. Fluorerscent lamps produce about four times as much light per watt as do incandescent bulbs.
- Turn off lights in rooms that aren't being used. Use outdoor lights only when they are needed. Clean lighting fixtures regularly; dust impairs their efficiency.
- Turn off television sets that aren't being watched. Turn off stereos, radios, irons and other appliances when not in use.
- When laundering, set the wash temperature selector to cold or warm as often as possible. Avoid overdrying the clothes. Clean the lint filter thoroughly after each load.
- Keep reflector pans beneath stovetop heating elements bright and clean. Shiny pans help focus heat on utensil bottoms; dull, soiled pans absorb heat.

- Never boil water in an open pan. Use close-fitting covers on pots and pans to retain heat.
- Use the dishwasher only when there is a full load. Let your dishes air dry, even if you wash them in a dishwasher.

Fuels of the Future

Decreasing dependency on fossil fuels while maintaining or improving living standards requires that we develop and use other energy sources. A variety of alternate energy sources exist. No single source is likely to meet all our energy needs. Some sources are limited to certain geographical locations. Others depend on limited resources. Together, however, they could end our need for fossils fuels.

Some alternatives to fossil fuels are currently providing significant amounts of energy and heat without causing major environmental problems. Others require time and money for research and development before they reach the point where they are technologically possible, environmentally attractive and economically feasible. And still others might best be discarded, for they have inherent flaws. Warns Denis Hayes of Stanford University, chairman of Earth Day 1990, "The 'solutions' we pursue for today's problems can create tomorrow's catastrophes."

Solar Power

Only a tiny fraction of the sun's radiation reaches the Earth. Yet our planet receives about 1 million times more energy from the sun than from all the U.S. power plants combined!

Using solar energy to produce heat and electricity has long been attractive to many people. Solar energy is nonpolluting, inexhaustible and readily available. It is free to anyone who has the equipment to use it. On the down side, solar energy cannot be collected at night or on cloudy days, so photoelectric cells or some other storage system is needed. Also, some places in the world do not receive enough sunshine during the year to make solar energy a viable energy source.

Solar technologies include photovoltaics, collectors and reflectors.

Photovoltaic cells change light energy directly into electric energy. The amount of electricity generated by each cell is small. Thus, many cells are needed to produce electricity in commercial quantities. Costs per watt are still high but falling rapidly. In the early 1970s, a photovoltaic cell capable of generating one watt of electricity cost more than $100; today the cost is under $4—and falling. (In contrast, oil-fired steam generators produce electricity for as little as 5 cents per kilowatt.)

Solar collectors, which are sometimes seen on the roofs of newer homes and other buildings, convert solar energy into heat. The collectors consist of blackened aluminum tubes that have water circulating in them. The sun's radiation heats the water as it moves through the tubes. This heated water can be used both for space heating and for hot water.

Solar reflector systems have large mirrors that reflect the sun's rays to a central point. This concentrates a great deal of heat on the point—heat that can be used in industrial processes or converted to electricity. The mirrors are movable and computer-controlled to track the sun.

One technology that uses huge curved mirrors arranged in long rows is the solar thermoelectric system. Each mirror has

RACING WITH THE SUN

The Sunraycer is a strange looking car: a streamlined single-seater with bicycle wheels and a set of fins above the driver's gold-lined canopy. But on a grueling trip across Australia, it averaged 43.5 miles an hour—without burning a single drop of gasoline!

The source of the Sunraycer's power is an array of 7,200 photovoltaic cells covering the back of the car. They convert 16.5% of the solar energy striking them into electrical energy. The energy powers a two-horsepower motor. Excess energy is stored in 68 silver-zinc batteries, for use during periods of reduced sunlight.

The Sunraycer made history in 1987, when it easily outraced 24 other solar-powered cars in the first World Solar Challenge. This 1,950-mile (3,138-kilometer) race from Darwin to Adelaide was organized by an Australian auto enthusiast.

Will solar-powered cars someday replace today's gas-guzzlers? It is doubtful that they will become economically attractive in the near future. "Still, as we all know, petroleum won't last forever," commented Jack R. Harned of General Motors, the company that built the Sunraycer.

The Need to Conserve Energy

a pipe running down its center. Within the pipe is an oil that absorbs and retains heat. On a sunny day, the temperature of the oil may reach temperatures above 700°F (371°C). As the hot oil passes through a heat exchanger, water in the exchanger turns to steam, which is used to drive a traditional turbine. The turbine generates electricity.

Solar thermoelectric plants in California's sunny Mojave Desert operated by Luz International had a total capacity of 275 megawatts in 1990. This is enough electricity to power the homes in a city the size of Miami or Cincinnati. But cloudy weather limits the plants' production. Still, the Luz plants are already playing an important role in southern California. They provide electricity to Los Angeles when the city needs it most: on hot sunny days when everyone is running an air conditioner.

Wind

Wind power is one of the world's oldest sources of energy. People have long used winds to power windmills and move ships on the sea. And since early in the 20th century, conversion systems have enabled people to change wind power into electricity.

In the past few decades, huge wind machines called turbine generators have been built. These have propeller-like rotors that usually exceed 75 feet (23 meters) in diameter. Smaller machines, suitable for use by individual homeowners, have also become available. What's more, when the wind is especially strong, these small-scale machines can be equipped to send excess electricity into the local utility's power system.

Some 90% of the wind-generated energy in the United States—and more than 70% of the world total—is produced in California. Hawaii follows, with several "wind farms" that provide more than 3% of that state's energy.

Windmills must be placed in an area exposed to winds, such as on a hilltop or near a large body of open water. One model, Boeing's MOD-5B, can generate 3,200 kilowatts of power at peak capacity. During one year, it produced electricity equivalent to that generated by 58,400 barrels of oil. This is enough electricity to meet the needs of up to 1,300 homes.

Biomass

Trees, grass, crops, manure, sewage and garbage are collectively referred to as biomass. At the present time, most biomass energy is derived from burning wood and wood wastes. But as communities run out of places to bury or dump their garbage, incinerating it to produce heat and electricity is becoming attractive. There is concern, however, about the emission of harmful chemicals by incinerators.

"Such incinerators produce major air pollution problems, and their hazardous ash constitutes a difficult disposal problem," says Denis Hayes. "Perhaps most important, incinerators create a strong vested interest in a continual flow of combustible trash. This can effectively destroy efforts at source reduction, recycling and composting—all preferable solutions to incineration. This is an instance where a bad solution can preclude better solutions."

Biomass can also be turned into fuel. For instance, ethyl alcohol (ethanol) can be produced by the fermentation of agricultural crop residues. Methyl alcohol (methanol) can be made from coal, wood or manure. These alcohols can be mixed with gasoline to produce a fuel called gasohol. Brazil, one of the world's largest producers of sugarcane, has been a leader in the development of gasohol. Sugarcane is used to make a 20%-alcohol gasohol. It is also used for a 100%-alcohol fuel. The alcohol fuel gives 17% less mileage than the gasohol. But because of subsidies from the Brazilian government, the alcohol is 40% cheaper to produce.

Gasohol is viewed more as a bridge to the future than as a solution to fossil fuel problems. It, too, produces significant amounts of pollution. Its primary value is to extend fossil fuel supplies until better alternatives are available.

Hydropower

Moving water is another power source used by people for thousands of years. But it was only after turbines and generators were invented in the 1800s that waterpower could be used to create electricity. Today, there are thousands of hydroelectric plants—combinations of turbines and electric generators—all over the world. In places where there is not enough moving water, people have built dams to trap water in artificial lakes called reservoirs. Water released from the reservoir passes through a hydroelectric plant combined with the dam to produce electricity.

There are tens of thousands of small dams that do not generate power. If hydroelectric plants were installed at some of these, significant amounts of energy could be produced.

Ocean Power

Ocean water can also be used to turn turbines to generate electricity. Several methods are being studied.

Ocean thermal energy conversion (OTEC) involves the use of warm surface waters to boil a liquid that has a low boiling point, such as ammonia or propane. The gas that is produced is used to drive a turbine. Then the gas is condensed back into a liquid to repeat the process.

The power of tides can be used to operate a hydroelectric plant in much the same way as the power of moving river water. A dam is built across a coastal inlet. Incoming tides pass through turbines in the dam to produce electricity and to fill a resevoir. When the tide drops, the water runs out of the inlet through the turbines, generating more electricity.

Similarly, the to-and-fro motion of waves can be used to drive turbines. Or waves could be channeled into a narrow trough, creating a mass of surging water to turn turbines.

Geothermal Energy

The Earth is a tremendous reservoir of heat, or geothermal energy. This energy is apparently created by the decay of radioactive material deep within the planet. It has been used by people for centuries, though generally on a small scale. The potential for large-scale use is significant, however. The energy source is virtually inexhaustible and is theoretically available anywhere.

There are three basic sources of geothermal energy: steam, hot water and hot dry rock.

Steam can be passed through turbines to generate electricity. The largest such plant in the world is north of San Francisco, California, at a natural steam field called The

Geysers. There, steam from the Earth has been used to produce electric power since 1960.

Hot water has been used mostly for heating purposes. Iceland is the most notable user of geothermal energy for heat. More than 80% of that nation's homes are heated by hot water from geothermal wells.

Hot dry rock offers the greatest potential source of geothermal energy. A technique similar to that used in petroleum recovery has been proposed to extract heat from hot rocks deep beneath the surface. Two deep wells are drilled. Millions of gallons of water are pumped down one well. The water absorbs heat from the hot rocks and is then forced at very high pressure up into the second well. When it reaches the surface, this superhot water is converted to steam.

Nuclear Energy

In a nuclear reactor, the nuclei of uranium atoms are split into smaller nuclei. In the process, called fission, energy is released. This nuclear energy is converted into heat energy, which can then be used to generate electricity.

Many billions of dollars have been spent by governments, particularly the U.S. government, to develop and promote nuclear energy—much, much more than has been spent on other alternatives to fossil fuels. Today, there are more than 100 nuclear energy plants in the United States. They produce about 7% of the energy consumed in the nation (as compared to 90% from fossil fuels). Nuclear plants provide an even greater portion of electric power in France and several other nations.

There is considerable opposition to nuclear power. People's major concern is the harmful effects of radiation on humans and other organisms. Radiation significantly increases the risk for cancer among people who are exposed to it, as well as increasing the risk of genetic damage to their children. The biggest fear is a major accident, such as occurred at Three Mile Island in Pennsylvania (1979) and, even worse, at Chernobyl in the Soviet Union (1986). But low-level emissions can also have major health impacts because the effect of radiation is cumulative. According to a study based on documents from

A SOLUTION CREATES A PROBLEM

Sometimes, solving one technological problem causes new problems. This occurred when the United States passed the Clean Air Act of 1970. Among the law's provisions were new standards for automobile emissions, limiting emissions of pollutants such as nitrogen oxides and hydrocarbons. How would automotive engineers meet this requirement?

The engineers solved the problem by developing a device called the catalytic converter. Installed in an automobile's exhaust system, it converts environmentally harmful gases into harmless gases. This occurs as the gases react with a chemical called a catalyst. A catalytic converter cuts carbon monoxide emissions 76%. It cuts nitrogen oxide and hydrocarbon emissions 96%.

But a new problem arose. At the time the catalytic converter was developed, gasoline contained lead. The lead additives improved gasoline efficiency, helping the gasoline burn properly in high-compression engines. But the lead additives could ruin the catalyst in the catalytic converter, as well as cause serious health problems.

Simply removing the lead additives wasn't enough. Gasoline without the additives didn't burn properly in the engines. It caused a knocking sound and harmed the engines.

The engineers took a step backward. They designed lower compression engines. The new engines do not burn gasoline as completely as higher compression engines. Their mileage is less. But they will burn gasoline without lead additives.

---

the U.S. Nuclear Regulatory Commission, there were 105,265 instances of worker exposure to measurable radiation at U.S. commercial nuclear reactors in 1988. Each exposed worker received an average dose that was roughly equivalent to 20 chest X rays.

Waste management is another problem. Nuclear fission produces long-lived radioactive wastes. Thousands of tons of such wastes exist, and finding a place to safely deposit them has been a thorny, unsolved problem.

Someday, we may have another source of nuclear energy: fusion. This is the process that releases the energy radiated by the sun. It also is the process used in hydrogen bombs. In fusion, energy is produced when two nuclei of a very light element combine, or fuse. Fusion reactors would be cleaner and safer than fission reactors. But much work needs to be done before such reactors are a reality. Fusion is still considered to be decades away from practical demonstration.

What Are the Risks?

Your community is encouraging carpooling by providing discounts on bridge tolls and establishing highway "fast lanes" for cars with more than two passengers. Should you join a car pool or use your own car? Being part of a car pool saves you money and limits greenhouse gas emissions. But you cannot be flexible with your working hours, nor can you run chores on the way home. Does the inconvenience outweigh the benefits? Or is the trade-off worthwhile?

The process of determining the adverse consequences that could result from some action is called risk assessment. It's playing an important role as people confront the effects of global warming.

Typically, risk assessment has three basic elements: What are the possible risks of an action or a new technology? What is the probability that a particular risk will occur? How many people, animals, lakes or other environmental components would be harmed if the risk occurred?

For example, your community's electrical demands are increasing. To meet them, a new source of energy is needed. Should the utility company build a coal-burning power plant? A nuclear power plant? What other options are available? What are the possible risks to your community of each option?

Uncertainty is often a factor in risk assessment. No one knows exactly how much respiratory damage is caused by pollutants released from a coal-burning power plant. It cannot be said that a certain nuclear power plant will ever release radiation into the environment.

Finally, there's the matter of trade-offs. Is an action worth the price? Is meeting your community's increasing electrical demands worth the possible risks of a coal-burning power plant? A nuclear plant or some other option? Who decides?

Weighing risks against benefits and making decisions becomes even more difficult when more than one community—or more than one nation—is involved. Many acres of tropical forests have been destroyed to create cattle ranches. The cattle provide meat used to make hamburgers for America's fast-food restaurants. Destroying the forests destroys habitats and increases global warming. But the ranches provide work and money for people, and the meat they produce helps keep down food prices in the United States. Are the long-term risks of such deforestation acceptable when compared to the current economic benefits provided by the ranches? Who decides?

11

SLOWING THE WARMING TREND

In addition to cutting our use of fossil fuels, other steps need to be taken to stabilize the greenhouse-gas content of the atmosphere and to limit global warming and ozone destruction.

Scientists and engineers have already developed numerous useful technologies in their efforts to reduce emissions. Many more technologies are under development. It is important to remember, however, that new technologies cannot be brought to the marketplace overnight. Often, several years or even decades are needed to bring a technology from its inception to the point where it is economically feasible and socially desirable. Photovoltaic cells, described in the previous chapter, are an example. The theory of photovoltaics has been understood since 1856. Serious development of photovoltaics didn't begin until 1954, however, when the concept became attractive as a means of providing electricity to orbiting satellites. At first, the price to generate electricity with photovoltaic cells was around $2,000 per watt. Today it is under $4 per watt. By the end of the 1990s, developers expect to be able to cut the cost to 50 cents per watt.

New Products and Processes

In thousands of laboratories around the world researchers are looking for clean, safe alternatives to products and processes that pollute the environment.

Opposite page: The way our products are packaged is clear evidence of our wasteful "throwaway" habits. New methods for packaging products and recycling waste must be developed if we are to slow the process of global warming.

> **WHO PAYS?**
>
> The cost of correcting our past environmental mistakes will be staggeringly high. Let's consider just one small part of the picture:
>
> Older power plants emit huge amounts of polluting gases, a practice that could be limited by installing scrubbers. The cost to refit large U.S. power plants with scrubbers has been estimated at some $50 billion. Who should pay for this? The power companies and their customers? Or everyone in the country?
>
> Instead of putting scrubbers in plants that will only last another 15 or 20 years, perhaps we should just wait until a technology to burn fuel more cleanly and efficiently is available. But when will that be? And will it be any cheaper than installing scrubbers? And who will pay for it?
>
> Another possibility would be to have power plants that burn high-sulfur coal (the most polluting kind) switch to low-sulfur coal. But this would idle thousands of coal miners in West Virginia, Kentucky, Ohio and Illinois. How would they be compensated?
>
> Or we could just gradually phase out the old power plants in 15 to 20 years. But can the environment wait that long? Often, even though the costs are high, the costs of inaction are much higher.

Ozone-Safe Refrigerants

Chemists are racing to find substitutes for CFCs, which are being phased out under an international agreement. One alternative is hydrofluorocarbons, or HFCs. These refrigerants do not contain chlorine and therefore are not expected to be a threat to ozone. In 1990, E.I. du Pont de Nemours & Company announced that it would build four plants to produce HFCs. When they become operational, the plants will have the capacity to supply most worldwide refrigeration needs through the end of the century.

However, HFCs are powerful greenhouse gases. An HFC molecule may absorb 2,500 times as much heat as a carbon dioxide molecule. Thus, while HFCs solve one problem, they exacerbate another.

Some companies are manufacturing refrigerators that do not rely on CFCs or HFCs. For example, Cryodynamics produces a refrigerator that cools with helium.

A Cleaner Cleaner

A CFC-free method for cleaning computer circuit boards has been developed by Digital Equipment Corporation. The water-based process uses a specially designed nozzle that sprays at constantly changing angles. This allows the cleaning solution to reach surfaces that previously were only accessible with CFCs.

No NO

Emissions of harmful gases can be reduced by installing systems to trap pollutants inside combustion chambers, smokestacks, and so on. For instance, in the United States, scrubbers that remove sulfur dioxide are required on most new utility and industrial boilers. Scrubbers remove, or "scrub out," sulfur dioxide by passing smoke through a mixture of limestone and water. They can remove about 95% of the sulfur dioxide, but at a cost: they consume about 5% of the energy produced by burning the coal, thereby increasing coal consumption; and they produce thousands of tons of waste.

There's an additional problem, too. The scrubbers do not trap nitrogen oxide (NO), which contributes to the formation of smog and acid rain. The problem: nitrogen oxide doesn't dissolve in water, so it passes through the mist of limestone and water used to trap the water-soluble sulfur dioxide. In 1990, chemists at Lawrence Berkeley Laboratory reported that the addition of phosphorus to the scrubbing mist may solve the problem. A series of reactions changes nitrogen oxide into water-soluble nitrogen dioxide (NO_2). The nitrogen dioxide then dissolves and can be removed in the same manner as the sulfur dioxide. In one experiment, the researchers were able to remove all of the sulfur dioxide—and all of the nitrogen oxide.

Millions of Trees

Halting deforestation would significantly reduce carbon dioxide emissions. In addition, it is necessary to reforest large areas. Ecologists Richard A. Houghton and George M. Woodwell of the Woods Hole Research Center have pointed out that the land is available:

"The reforestation of from 1 to 2 million square kilometers (about the area of Alaska) will result in the annual storage of one billion tons of carbon. Although this area is large and productive land in the Tropics is at a premium, there may be as much as 8.5 million square kilometers of once forested land available for reforestation. Of this land, about 3.5 million square kilometers could be returned to forest if permanent agriculture were to replace shifting cultivation. Another five million square kilometers of deforested land are currently unused, and there reforestation could in principle be implemented immediately. Forests established to store carbon would, of course, have to be maintained: neither harvested nor destroyed by toxic effects or change in climate."

In his 1990 State of the Union address, U.S. President George Bush proposed the planting of a billion trees a year for several years "to help keep this country clean, from our forestland to the inner cities." The program would be administered by the U.S. Forest Service, which would plant and maintain 970 million trees on rural lands and 30 million trees in communities annually. Many of the trees would be planted on existing forestlands. U.S. Department of Agriculture sur-

OUT WITH THE OLD, IN WITH THE NEW?

Young trees grow faster than old trees. Thus, a forest of young trees removes more carbon dioxide from the atmosphere each year than a forest of old trees. Therefore, say some people in the logging industry, let's replace old-growth forests with fast-growing young trees.

Furthermore, they say, by cutting down the old trees and using the wood in buildings and other products, the trees don't die, decompose and release carbon dioxide into the atmosphere.

Do logging proponents have a valid argument? Not according to Mark E. Harmon and William K. Ferrell of Oregon State University and Jerry F. Franklin of the University of Washington. These scientists found major errors in the argument.

First, old trees store much more carbon than young trees. The scientists used a computer model to compare total carbon storage in a 60-year-old hemlock forest and a 450-year-old forest of hemlocks and Douglas fir (the type of forest common in the Pacific Northwest). The older forest held more than twice as much carbon. Furthermore, it takes at least 200 years for the storage capacity of a replanted forest to approach that of an old-growth forest.

Second, the scientists found that less than half of the timber harvested in the Pacific Northwest is stored in long-lasting products (defined as products with a life span of more than five years). Large portions are burned or turned into paper and wood chips. These products rapidly decompose and release carbon dioxide. The result, noted the scientists, is that for every 100 grams of carbon harvested from a typical old-growth forest, 57 grams may be lost to the atmosphere in a few years. No wonder, then, that the scientists found that the logging of old-growth forests in the Pacific Northwest "has been a significant source" of carbon in the atmosphere.

---

veys indicate that up to 80 million acres (32 million hectares) of private, nonindustrial woodlands are in poor condition. "Tree planting and [other] practices that promote the natural regeneration of forests can bring such nonstocked and understocked stands back into healthy condition," point out government forestry experts.

Individual Action

Individuals also have many important roles to play in the battle to control greenhouse warming. "I believe that we human beings have an ethical obligation to practice environmental reciprocity—to protect, nourish and sustain the natural systems that protect, nourish and sustain us. Doing so is not just a job for government, or business, or farmers or conservationists—it's a job for all of us," stresses William K. Reilly, head of the U.S. Environmental Protection Agency.

Plant a Tree

There are an estimated 100 million available tree-planting spaces around homes and businesses in U.S. towns and cities. Some fast-growing trees use carbon dioxide at the rate of about 48 pounds (22 kilograms) per year—approximately 10 tons per acre. As the American Forestry Association points out, "put another way, for every ton of new wood that grows, about 1.47 tons of carbon dioxide are removed from the air."

Recycle Paper

If Americans recycled all their Sunday newspapers, they would save more than 500,000 trees a week! Even better than recycling is reusing. Reuse manila envelopes by placing new address labels atop the old. Use the back side of junk mail printed on only one side as scrap paper. Turn the comic pages into gift wrap. The list of possibilities is almost endless.

Maintain the A/C

If you feel you must have air-conditioning in your car, be sure to maintain it properly. To avoid leaks of the coolant (which contains CFCs) run the air conditioner once a month during the winter. This prevents hoses from drying and cracking. Have the air conditioner checked regularly and fix leaks promptly. Don't just pour in a do-it-yourself can of refrigerant. The CFCs you put in today will be in the atmosphere next week.

Write Your Government Representatives

Express your concern over policies that encourage wasteful practices and that discourage efforts to protect the atmosphere. Urge action on reducing emissions of carbon dioxide and other industrial gases. Give specific examples of steps you recommend. For instance, you might suggest tax credits to encourage the use and development of solar heating.

Governmental Action

Almost every developed nation has or is formulating plans to reduce its contributions to global warming. For example, the

Netherlands plans a reduction in carbon dioxide emissions so that by 1994–95 those emissions will be stabilized at 1989–90 levels. Continued reductions are planned for succeeding years. In addition, the nation is committed to an 85% reduction in CFC emissions by 1995 and a total phaseout of these chemicals by 1998.

To meet its target reductions in carbon dioxide emissions, the Netherlands is developing a broad range of measures. These include a tax on carbon dioxide emissions, tightened building-code standards for insulation, energy-efficiency standards for appliances, subsidies for residential and industrial energy-conservation programs, and matching funds for relevant research and development.

Developing nations are caught between responding to the greenhouse threat and meeting other needs viewed as more pressing. Comments Dilip R. Ahuja of India's Tata Energy Research Institute: "Realistically, given India's chronic shortages of electricity and unmet demands for energy services, it is unlikely that greenhouse-gas emissions from the energy sector will be reduced in the near future. Most credible projections indicate that these emissions will grow at an average annual rate of nearly 4 percent, quadrupling over the next 40 years."

Even developing nations are beginning to recognize, however, that it is not to their advantage to allow their forests to be destroyed, their fish to be killed by acid rain, their cities to be shrouded in smog. In Brazil, the space and environmental agencies are cooperating in a fire-prevention program to prevent illegal burning of the Amazon rain forest. "In 1988–89 satellite images were used to detect fires, and helicopters were dispatched to check for clearing permits; fines were imposed on violators. During this period, deforestation in the Brazilian Amazon declined by an estimated 30%, at least in part as a result of this program."

Global Action

Many remedies for limiting global warming require international action. Individual efforts and domestic legislation are inadequate to deal with problems that transcend borders. When a power plant in the American Midwest spews out pollutants, it affects not only the local environment but also environments thousands of miles away, in other states, in other countries. When rain forests in Brazil are hacked down, the carbon dioxide that is emitted spreads around the world, to affect climates everywhere.

"The world cannot afford to rely on independent action by individual countries," notes Elliot L. Richardson, who headed the U.S. delegation to the Law of the Sea Conference from 1977 to 1980. "The results are bound to be highly uneven: One nation could cut back on its carbon dioxide emissions; one could stop the destruction of its own forests; still another could do nothing. The least responsible transnational corporations will seek out and encourage the most permissive regulatory environments."

International Agreements

Global warming is likely to be a major world political issue in the coming years as nations try to agree on solutions that are equitable to all. Some actions have already been taken:

In 1987, 24 nations and the European Community signed the Montreal Protocol on Substances that Deplete the Ozone

ARCTIC FINGERPRINTS

A massive cloud of pollution sat atop the Arctic. Where did it come from? The United States, the Soviet Union, Canada, Iceland and the Scandinavian countries all touch the Arctic. Which country was responsible for producing this mess?

Today, scientists can use lasers and other equipment to trace pollution to its source. This is an important step in dealing with people who say such things as, "You can't prove that my factory is polluting your town" or "The acid rain that's killing your trees isn't caused by my country."

Just as a fingerprint is unique to one individual, each air mass is unique. It contains a distinctive mixture of gases and particles. Scientists examined samples of air from the Arctic cloud. They found a combination that included arsenic, selenium, antimony and indium. It was a combination likely to be produced in a smelting area in the Ural Mountains of the Soviet Union. They also found dry-cleaning chemicals and other substances commonly used by Soviets but seldom used in Western nations. Based on this "fingerprinting," the scientists concluded that the cloud of polluted air had to come from the Soviet Union.

Although this particular cloud originated in the Soviet Union, others are formed worldwide, in both industrialized and developing countries. With "fingerprinting," these countries will not be able to deny responsibility, either.

Layer. In the years that followed, additional nations signed the agreement, which established a series of deadlines that would reduce CFC production 50% by 1998. In 1989, the 12 European Community countries decided to phase out CFCs entirely by the end of the century.

In 1990, heeding scientists' calls for greater action to protect the ozone layer, representatives of 93 nations met in London and agreed to stop production of CFCs by the end of the decade. The agreement also ends the production of three halons, heat-trapping chemicals that are used in fire extinguishers. And it sharply restricts production of methyl chloroform and carbon tetrachloride, both of which contain chlorine. Developing nations were given a 10-year grace period, and a fund was set up to help these nations make the transition to more suitable technologies.

In 1989, 67 countries and 11 international organizations met in Noordwijk, the Netherlands. The result was the Noordwijk Declaration on Climate Change, which called for a stabilization of carbon dioxide emissions as soon as possible. Target dates and stabilization levels were to be addressed at a later world climate conference.

Some people have suggested the creation of a separate United Nations agency to deal with global warming. Also, there is a need for an international treaty or some other mechanism to enforce regulations.

International Assistance

It is important that developing nations become convinced that protecting their environments and limiting their use of fossil fuels is in their own best interests. Industrialized nations have the technological and financial resources to help these nations find ways to improve living standards without massive environmental degradation. Collaboration between the two groups is essential. For instance, tropical countries can be helped to exploit solar energy as an alternative to fossil fuels. They can be encouraged to create forest management plans that ensure that the forests will provide sustained yields of wood throughout the coming years. They can be given financial assistance to install anti-pollution devices.

Is It Really Happening?

Despite increasing evidence, there remain people who say that global warming is a fantasy. That it won't happen. Or if it does, that negative climatic feedbacks will hold it to negligible levels. So, they say, all the headlines, all the pressure to change our life-styles, our habits, our industrial and agricultural practices is unnecessary. Besides, they point out, scientists don't agree, so let's not worry about doing anything until we know for certain that warming is occurring.

"The relevant policy question is not whether the scientists are right but whether policy makers can afford to be wrong," commented U.S. Congressman James H. Scheuer. The nature of global warming is such that if we wait until its impacts are obvious, it may be too late for science and technology to bail us out. The sooner we act, the more resolutely we act, the better our chances of lessening the degree of warming.

Scheuer points out that there are additional benefits to be gained from limiting greenhouse-gas emissions: "Suppose we take reasonable, cost-effective steps to slow down global warming, and learn later the scientists were wrong and we didn't have to do anything after all. Admittedly, we will have spent billions of dollars to reduce emissions of greenhouse gases. But, wisely spent, that investment will have brought us billions of dollars of benefits: reduced pollution, improved health, more energy-efficient cars, U.S. industry that is more internationally competitive, and the creation of new global markets for American-made environmental technologies and services."

Scheuer was speaking to Americans when he made these comments. But his points are valid for people everywhere. The uncertainties that must be resolved by scientists are admittedly great. But there will probably always be uncertainties, for we are dealing with extremely complex natural processes. It is important to remember that despite the uncertainties, scientists are generally agreed that global warming is happening and will continue to happen, and that its impact on the Earth and all the organisms that inhabit this precious planet will increase. How great that impact will be is up to us.

GLOSSARY

acid rain precipitation polluted by acids, particularly sulfuric and nitric acids.
atmosphere the air surrounding a planet.
atom the smallest particle of matter that has all the characteristics of a chemical element; when two or more atoms combine, they form molecules.
carbon dioxide (CO_2) a common carbon compound present in the atmosphere in increasing amounts due largely to human activities such as the burning of fossil fuels.
catalyst a substance that initiates a reaction or changes the speed of a reaction without being changed by the process.
CFCs (chlorofluorocarbons) man-made gases that are responsible for much of the destruction of the ozone layer.
climate the average weather condition in a region over a long period of time.
climatologist a scientist who studies long-term changes in weather patterns.
cloud condensation nuclei dust and other particles in the atmosphere around which water vapor condenses to form cloud particles.
condensation the changing of a gas to a liquid.
conservation measures to preserve natural resources, such as fossil fuels and forests.
deforestation the clearing away of a forest.
drought a long period of time without adequate precipitation.
ecologist a scientist who studies the relationships between organisms and their environments.
ecosystem a community of plants, animals and other organisms together with its physical environment.
emission material discharged into the environment.
evaporation changing of a liquid to a gas.
exosphere the region of very thin air beyond the thermosphere, extending from a height of about 300 miles (483 kilometers) and "blending" into space.
feedback a self-regulating mechanism that controls the rate or magnitude of a process.
fossil fuels coal, oil and natural gas, formed from the remains of organisms that lived millions of years ago.
geothermal energy heat energy created deep within the Earth.
glacier large, thick mass of slow-moving ice.
global circulation model (GCM) a complex computer program that simulates the interaction of physical processes in the atmosphere.
gravity an invisible force by which objects—such as the Earth and atmospheric particles—are pulled toward one another.
greenhouse effect the absorption of energy radiated from the Earth's surface by carbon dioxide and other gases in the atmosphere, causing the atmosphere to become warmer.
heat wave a period of unusually hot weather.
ice age a long period of time when glaciers, especially in the form of great ice sheets, cover large areas of the Earth.
industrial revolution the transformation to a mechanized society, with large-scale production facilities, that began in England about 1760.

infrared radiation an invisible form of long-wave radiation that has a heating effect.
mesosphere the layer of the atmosphere above the stratosphere, extending from a height of about 30 miles (48 kilometers) to about 53 miles (85 kilometers).
meteorologist a scientist who studies the weather.
molecule two or more atoms bound together by electrical charges; the smallest part of a compound that has all the characteristics of the compound.
nitrogen the most plentiful gas in the atmosphere.
nuclear fission the splitting of atomic nuclei, which produces large amounts of heat energy.
nuclear fusion the combination of small atomic nuclei to form heavier atoms, which produces large amounts of heat energy.
oxygen (O_2) the second most plentiful gas in the atmosphere; needed by plants and animals for respiration.
ozone (O_3) a form of oxygen present primarily in the stratosphere and responsible for blocking ultraviolet radiation.
ozone hole a region in the stratosphere of depleted ozone levels.
photosynthesis the process by which green plants make food.
precipitation water that falls from clouds in the form of rain, snow, sleet or hail.
reforestation replanting previously forested areas with trees.
risk assessment the process of determining the adverse consequences that could result from some action or technology.
sea level the average water level of the oceans.
smog a mixture of smoke and fog.
solar energy energy obtained from the sun.
storm surge a sudden onrush of massive amounts of water caused by a hurricane or other major storm.
stratosphere the layer of the atmosphere extending upward from the troposphere, from a height of about 6.8 miles (11 kilometers) to about 30 miles (48 kilometers).
thermosphere the layer of the atmosphere extending upward from the mesosphere, from a height of about 53 miles (85 kilometers) to about 300 miles (483 kilometers).
trace gases gases present in very small amounts.
troposphere the layer of the atmosphere nearest the Earth, extending to a height of about 6.8 miles (11 kilometers).
ultraviolet radiation an invisible form of short-wave radiation emitted by the sun.
water vapor the gaseous form of water.
weather the condition of the atmosphere at a particular place and time, in terms of temperature, pressure, wind and moisture.

FURTHER READING

Abrahamson, Dean Edwin (ed). *The Challenge of Global Warming.* Washington: Island Press, 1989.

Anzovin, Steven (ed). *Preserving the World Ecology.* New York: The H.W. Wilson Company, 1990.

Brown, Lester R., et al. *State of the World 1990.* New York: W.W. Norton & Company, 1990.

Environmental Defense Fund. *Protecting the Ozone Layer: What You Can Do.* New York: Environmental Defense Fund, 1988.

Erickson, Jon. *Greenhouse Earth: Tomorrow's Disaster Today.* Blue Ridge Summit, PA: Tab Books, 1990.

Flavin, Christopher. "Slowing Global Warming: A Worldwide Strategy." Worldwatch Paper No. 91. Washington: Worldwatch Institute, 1989.

Gay, Kathlyn. *The Greenhouse Effect.* New York: Franklin Watts, 1986.

Goldsmith, Edward, and Nicholas Hildyard (eds). *The Earth Report: The Essential Guide to Global Ecological Issues.* Los Angeles: Price Stern Sloan, 1988.

Gribben, John. *Future Weather and the Greenhouse Effect.* New York: Delacorte Press, 1982.

Gribben, John. *The Hole in the Sky.* New York: Bantam Books, 1988.

Lamb, Marjorie. *2 Minutes a Day for a Greener Planet.* San Francisco: Harper & Row, 1990.

Milne, Antony. *Our Drowning World: Population, Pollution and Future Weather* (2nd ed.). Garden City Park, NY: Avery Publishing Group, 1990.

National Research Council. *Ozone Depletion, Greenhouse Gases, and Climate Change.* Washington: National Academy Press, 1989.

Oppenheimer, Michael, and Robert H. Boyle. *Dead Heat: The Race against the Greenhouse Effect.* New York: Basic Books, 1990.

Roan, Sharon L. *Ozone Crisis: the 15-Year Evolution of a Sudden Global Emergency.* New York: John Wiley & Sons, 1989.

Schneider, Stephen H. *Global Warming: Are We Entering the Greenhouse Century?* San Francisco: Sierra Club Books, 1989.

Steger, Will, and Jon Bowermaster. *Saving the Earth: A Citizen's Guide to Environmental Action.* New York: Alfred A. Knopf, 1990.

In addition, the following publications regularly cover issues associated with global warming:

Amicus Journal. National Resources Defense Council, 40 West 20 Street, New York, NY 10011.
Atmosphere. Friends of the Earth. 701-251 Laurier Avenue West, Ottawa, Ontario K1P 5J6, Canada.
Environment. Heldref Publications, 1730 M L King Jr. Way, Berkeley, CA 94709.
Environmental Action. Environmental Action, Inc., 1525 New Hampshire, Washington, D.C. 20036.
EPA Journal. U.S. Environmental Protection Agency. Superintendent of Documents, GPO, Washington, DC 20402.
Greenpeace. Greenpeace USA, 1436 U Street, NW, Washington, DC 20009.
Natural History. American Museum of Natural History, Central Park West at 79th Street, New York, NY 10024.
Science. American Association for the Advancement of Science, 1333 H Street NW, Washington, D.C. 20005.
Science News. Science Service, 1719 N Street NW, Washington, D.C. 20036.
Sierra. Sierra Club, 730 Polk Street, San Francisco, CA 94109.
World Watch. Worldwatch Institute, 1776 Massachusetts Avenue, NW, Washington, D.C. 20036.

Directories of government agencies and private organizations concerned with environmental issues:

Conservation Directory. National Wildlife Federation, 8925 Leesburg Pike, Vienna, VA 22184.
Directory of Environmental Organizations. Educational Communications, Box 35473, Los Angeles, CA 90035.
Directory of National Environmental Organizations. U.S. Environmental Directories, Box 65156, St Paul, MN 55165.

INDEX

A
Acid rain, 29-31, 99
Adams, Richard M., 66
Agriculture. *See* Farming
Ahuja, Dilip R., 102
Air-conditioning, 79, 87, 101
Aluminum, 30, 83
Amazon rain forest, 22, 28-29, 102
Animals, 12, 23, 64, 79
Antarctica, 41-43, 47, 50, 60, 70
Appliances, efficiency of, 85, 86-87
Arctic, 71, 103
Argon, 12
Atlantic Coast, 61
Atlantic Ocean, 29, 59, 61
Atmosphere
  gases of, 11-14, 30
  layers of, 17-19
  seasons and, 32, 42
  study of, 13, 42-43
Atoms, 22
Australia, 51
Automobiles, 81, 83, 84, 89, 94

B
Balloons, weather, 13
Bangladesh, 62, 69
Barometer, 13
Beach erosion, 61
Biomass, 91
Birth defects, 93
Birth rate, 32
Black blizzards, 65
Bleviss, Deborah, 83
Bort, Teisserenc de, 13
Brazil, 29, 91, 102
British Antarctic Survey, 42-43
Bruck, Robert I., 31
Buildings, efficiency of, 84-85
Bush, George, 99

C
California, 67, 70, 78, 90
Cancer, 46, 93
Carbon dioxide
  atmospheric, 12, 50, 52, 59, 63
  clouds and, 54-55
  conservation and, 85-87, 102
  ice and, 49-50
  oceans and, 24-25, 53
  people and, 27-33
  plants and, 14, 21-24, 32, 63, 65-66, 86, 100, 101
Caribbean Sea, 59
Catalyst, 44
Catalytic converter, 94
Chandler, William U., 83
Charleston, SC, 62
Chemical elements, 22
Chernobyl, Soviet Union, 93
China, 82
Chlorine, 45
Chloroflurocarbons (CFCs), 38-39, 45-46, 98, 101, 102, 104
Chlorophyll, 22
Christy, John R., 51, 52
Cincinnati, OH, 65
Cities, 29
Clean Air Act (1970), 94
Climate models, 52
Clouds, 37, 54-55, 59
Coal, 24, 27, 29, 81, 82
Coastal areas, 61-62, 74-75
Coca production, 30
Combustion, 13
Compounds, chemical, 22
Computers, 52, 98
Conservation, energy, 81-95
Cosmic rays, 11

D
Dallas, TX, 60
Deforestation, 28-31, 95, 99, 102
Delaware River, 67
Desalination, 78-79
Dikes, 75
Dissociation, 44
Dourojeanni, Marc, 30
Droughts, 65, 66, 67, 70, 76
Dust particles, 15-16, 17
Dust storms, 16, 65

E
Ecological zones, 63, 64
Ecosystems, 47
Ecuador, 51
Efficiency, tips on, 84-88
Egypt, 62
E.I du Pont de Nemours & Company, 98
Electricity
  conservation and, 84, 86-90, 92, 93
  fuel and, 82
  temperature and, 79
Elements, chemical, 22
El Niño, 51
Energy conservation, 81-95
Environmental Protection Agency (EPA), 46, 61, 63, 65, 66
Erosion, 16, 61
Ethanol, 91
Europe, 70, 103-104
Exosphere, 19
Eye cataracts, 46-47

F
Farming, 64-68, 69, 75-79
Federal Bureau of Reclamation, 78
Feedback mechanisms, 54-55, 59
Ferrell, William K., 100
Floods, 70
Florida, 63
Forests, 22, 28-31, 63-64, 95, 99-100
Fossil fuels, 27-28, 29, 33, 52, 81, 82, 88
Franklin, Jerry F., 100
Freon, 30
Fuel efficiency, 83, 84, 88-94
Fusion, 94

G
Galilei, Galileo, 13
Gas
  atmospheric, 11-14, 30
  natural, 24, 27, 38, 81, 82
  refrigerator, 38-39
Gasohol, 91
Genetic defects, 93
Genetic engineering, 76
Geothermal energy, 92-93
Glacial rebounds, 71
Glaciers, 60, 70-71
Global circulation models (GCMs), 52-53, 58-59
Glucose, 21, 22, 23
Gore, Albert, Jr., 50
Government action, U.S., 83, 101-103

Great Britain, 70
Greeks, 13
Greenhouse effect, 6, 25, 53-54, 70, 105
Greenland, 49-50, 58, 60
Gulf of Mexico, 61, 62

H
Halley Bay, Antarctica, 42-43
Hansen, James E., 51, 53, 70
Harmon, Mark E., 100
Harned, Jack R., 89
Hartford, CT, 65
Hawaii, 90
Hayes, Denis, 88, 91
Health problems, 18, 46-47, 69, 71, 93
Heat energy
  carbon dioxide and, 21, 25, 27
  cities and, 29
  conservation and, 88-90, 92-93
Heat traps, 35-39
Helstra, Gjerrot P., 75
Herzog, Arthur, 60
Hoffman, John, 46
Home energy-saving tips, 86-87
Honolulu, HI, 61
Houghton, Richard A., 99
Humidity, 14, 59
Hurricanes, 59, 61, 70
Hydroflurocarbons (HFCs), 98
Hydrogen, 22
Hydropower, 91-92
Hydroxyl radical, 39

I
Ice age, predictions about, 59
Iceland, 58, 93
Ice studies, 47-48, 55, 60-61
Immune system diseases, 47, 69
Incinerators, 91
India, 29, 102
Indonesia, 29, 51
Industrial revolution, 33
Industry, 27-28, 33, 81, 98
Infrared radiation, 35
International agreements, 102-104
Irrigation, 67, 77
Isaksen, Ivar S.A., 47
Israel, 76, 78

J
Jet stream, 13
Jones, Philip D., 51

K
Keeler, Andrew A., 65
Keeling, Charles D., 33
Kenya, 71
Kettering, Charles F., 49
Krakatoa, Java, 17
Kudzu, 7

L
Labrador, 58
Landscaping, 86
La Niña, 51
Lashoff, Daniel A., 55
Leslie, Robert C., 37
Light
  artificial, 85-86
  plants and, 22
  visible, 44
  waves of, 11
Logging, 100
Los Angeles, CA, 5, 45, 68, 90
Louisiana, 61, 63
Louisville, KY, 29
Lovejoy, Thomas, 7
Low-energy precision application (LEPA), 77

M
Maine, 74
Malaria, 71
Mars, 25
Mauna Loa, HI, 33
Medieval Warm Period, 57-58
Mediterranean Sea, 58, 62
Memphis, TN, 60
Mesosphere, 19
Methane, 36-38, 50
Methanol, 91
Mexico, 45, 51
Microwave radiation, 52
Middle East, 79
Midwest, U.S., 58, 64, 65, 69, 70, 103
Migration, 79
Milankovitch, Milutin, 59
Mill Creek people, 58
Milliman, John D., 62
Missouri River, 67
Mitchell, J. Murray, Jr., 82
Molecules, 22, 39
Monsoons, 61
Mount Mitchell, NC, 31
Mount St. Helens, WA, 16
Murphy, Dennis, 64

N
National Academy of Sciences, 73, 74
National Aeronautics and Space Administration (NASA), 42
Native Americans, 58
Netherlands, 75, 102
New York, NY, 60, 79
Nile River, 58, 62
Nitrates, 12
Nitric oxide, 44-45
Nitrogen, 12, 44
Nitrogen dioxide, 44-45, 99
Nitrogen oxides, 29, 98-99
Nitrous oxide (laughing gas), 35-36, 85
North Carolina, 61
Northwest, U.S., 100
Nuclear energy, 93-94

O
Oceans
  carbon dioxide and, 24-25, 53
  energy and, 92
  forests and, 29
  temperature and, 51, 59, 60-61, 71
Ocean thermal energy conversion (OTEC), 92
Ogallala Aquifer, 67
Oil (fuel), 24, 27, 29, 81
Olivero, John J., 37
Othieno, Herik, 71
Oxygen
  function of, 12-13
  ozone and, 43-45
  people and, 27
  plants and, 22, 23
Ozone
  CFC's and, 39, 98, 103-104
  forests and, 31
  function of, 18, 19
  thinning of, 41-47, 69

P
Pacific Coast, 63
Pacific Ocean, 51
Pakistan, 78
Palermo, Sicily, 58
Paper recycling, 101
Peltier, W. Richard, 71
Peru, 30, 51
Peterson, Dean F., 64
Petroleum, 24
Philadelphia, PA, 67
Phoenix, AZ, 5, 68, 70
Photosynthesis, 22-23, 47

Photovoltaic cells, 89, 97
Phytoplankton, 47
Pietrafesa, Leonard J., 61
Plants
   carbon dioxide and, 14, 21-24, 32, 63, 65-66, 86, 100, 101
   endangered, 30-31, 47, 63-64, 79
   genetics and, 76
   nitrogen and, 12
   radiation and, 47
Polar zones, 58, 63
Population growth, 31-33
Postel, Sandra, 67, 68, 77-78
Proteins, 12

R
Radiation
   clouds and, 54-55
   function of, 15, 18, 35
   harm of, 18, 46-47, 93-94
   ozone and, 41, 44-47
   temperature and, 52, 59
Radicals, 39
Radiosonde, 13
Rainfall, 64-65
Rain forests, 22, 28-29, 30, 95, 102, 103
Recombinant-DNA, 76
Reilly, William K., 84, 100
Respiration, 13, 14, 23
Respiratory problems, 69
Richardson, Elliot, 103
Rind, David, 59
Risk assessment, 94-95
Russell, Rollo, 17

S
Sadik, Nafis, 32-33
Sagan, Carl, 39
San Bernadino Mountains, CA, 31
Satellites
   communication, 19
   weather, 13, 42, 51-52

Scheuer, James H., 105
Schneider, Claudine, 85, 86
Scrubbers, 98
Sea. *See* Oceans
Seasons, 32, 42
Sewage, 78
Shukla, Jagadish, 29
Skin Cancer, 46
Smith, Joel B., 74, 79
Smog, 29, 45, 99
Snow studies, 55
Solar power, 88-90
Solar radiation, 11, 14-15, 29, 46, 54-55, 59
Sound waves, 11
South Dakota, 67
Southeast, U.S., 65
Southwest, U.S., 5, 64-65
Soviet Union, 65, 102
Spencer, Roy W., 51, 52
Stars, shooting, 11
Storm surges, 62
Stratosphere, 18-19, 37, 39, 43, 45
Sulfur dioxide, 29-30, 85, 98, 99
Sun, 14, 22, 44, 46, 59, 88-90
Sunraycer car, 89

T
Temperature zones, 58, 63
Temperature
   average, 6
   cities and, 29
   effects of, 57-71
   oceans and, 25
   planets and, 25
   studies of, 50-55
Teramura, Alan F., 47
Texas, 5, 77
Theophrastus, 13
Thermal expansion, 60
Thermoelectric plants, 90
Thermometer, 13
Thermosphere, 19

Three Mile Island, PA, 93
Tiber River, 58
Timeline, 8-9
TIROS satellites, 13, 51
Töpfer, Klaus, 9
Torricelli, Evangelista, 13
Trace gases, 12
Trees, 31, 86, 99-100, 101
Tropical forest. *See* Rain forest
Troposphere, 17-18
Tushingham, A. Mark, 71

U
Ultraviolet radiation
   harm of, 18, 46-47
   ozone and, 44-47
   plants and, 66
United Nations, 31-33, 62, 104

V
Venus, 25
Vikings, 58
Volcanoes, 16-17, 33

W
Washington, D.C., 60
Washington, Warren M., 54
Water
   conservation of, 75, 76-79
   energy and, 91-92, 93
   oceans and, 24-25
   plants and, 22, 23
   shortage of, 67-68
   vapor and, 12, 14
Weather
   forecasting of, 13, 52
   formation of, 18
   patterns of, 7, 58-60
Wetlands, 62-63
White light, 44
Widgley, Thomas, Jr., 38
Wind, 16, 90
Wind storms, 70
Woodwell, George M., 99

Photo Credits

Page 4, Barry L. Runk/Grant Heilman; p.7, ©David M. Dennis/Tom Stack Associates; p.10, U.S.G.S.; p.20, Al Lowry/ Photo Researchers, Inc.; p.26, Michael Hanulak/Photo Researchers, Inc.; p.34, ©Reneé Lynn/ Photo Researchers, Inc.; p.40, Documerica/Flip Schulke, National Archive; p.46, © Blackbirch Graphics, Inc.,p.48, NASA; p.56, ©Keith Gunnar/ Photo Researchers, Inc.; p.68, AP/Wide World; p.72, Alexander Lowry/ Photo Researchers, Inc.; p.75, The British Museum; p.80, ©Tom McHugh/ Photo Researchers, Inc.; p.96, ©Greg Vaughn/ Tom Stack Associates.

Cover,opener to Problems, © Jeff Foott/Tom Stack Associates; portfolio page 2, © David M. Doody/Tom Stack Associates; portfolio page 3, © Robert Winslow/ Tom Stack Associates; portfolio page 4, (top) Ken Karp, (bottom), Grant Heilman; portfolio page 5,© Blackbirch Graphics, Inc.;portfolio page 6,©Brian Parker/ Tom Stack Associates; page 7, Carl Purcell/ Science Source/ Photo Researchers, Inc.;page 8, © Michael P. Gadomski/ Photo Researchers, Inc. Portfolio, Solutions:Opener, Larry Le Fever/ Grant Heilman; pages 2-3, © Kevin Schaefer/ Tom Stack Associates; page 4, Owens Corning; page 5, © Jeff Le Pore/ Photo Researchers, Inc.; pages 6-7, © Hank Morgan/ Photo Researchers, Inc.;page 8, © Lowell Georgia/ Photo Researchers, Inc.

Photo Research by **Photosearch, Inc.**